Stunt Kites!

edited by
David Gomberg

cover illustration by Kathleen Brady

with comments and contributions by:
Bill Baker, Cris Batdorff, Rick Bell, Eric Forsberg,
Susan Gomberg, Rod Guyette, Bob Hanson, Al Hargus III,
Corey Jensen, Robert Loera, Ray & Jeanne Merry,
Abel Ortega, Ron Reich, Marti Sasaski,
Lee Sedgwick, Robbi Sugarman, Sue Taft,
and Eric & Dorothy Wolff

Table of Contents

Thanks again to those who have offered
comments and contributions to this effort:

Bill Baker - Peter Powell Kites
Cris Batdorff - Stunt Kite Quarterly Magazine
Rick Bell - San Diego
Eric Forsberg - AKA Stunt Kite Committeee
Susan Gomberg - Cascade Kites
Rod Guyette - Ramjet Kites
Bob Hanson - Stunt Kite Quarterly Magazine
Al Hargus III - Dragons & Butterflies Productions
Corey Jensen - Windborne Kites
Robert Loera - Kite Fantasy
Ray & Jeanne Merry - Cobra Kites/Flexifoil International
Abel Ortega - Stinger Kites
Ron Reich - San Diego
Marti Sasaski - Sasaski Kite Fabrications
Lee Sedgwick - Team High Fly
Robbi Sugarman - Air Circus
Sue Taft - Team High Fly
Eric & Dorothy Wolff - Chicago Fire

and the hundreds of other flyers
that I have talked to,
flown with,
and learned from.

Introduction

This is a book about flying stunt kites.

We don't talk about kite history or how to make kites. What we've done is try to produce the "Complete Flying Manual".

There are now hundreds of different and distinct stunt kites being manufactured and distributed. Regional and national events attracting thousands of spectators are held around the country and around the world.

Whether you're a new pilot or an experienced competitor, we've tried to compile the basic or technical information you're looking for along with specialized tips to improve performance. We've also worked to update the text each year with new techniques or developments.

Within these pages, you'll find comments and contributions by some of the best flyers in the world.

> -- In Chapter One, we explain how the wind affects kite flying and how to pick a flying site.
> -- In Chapers Two thru Four, we provide basic instructions for the new flyer.
> -- Chapter Five is an overview of tuning - one of the most confusing and least understood aspects of kite performance.
> -- Chapter Seven explains all about the different types of flylines and how to take care of them.
> -- Chapter Eight covers exotic , new, or different techniques - everything from "power flying" to flying backwards through a dog stake.
> -- Finally, in Chapter Nine, we present information on stunt kite contests with specific tips on how to improve your scores.

The most important thing is that we want to promote safe and responsible flying.

Stunt kites and stunt kiting are evolving on a daily basis. That's one reason we have not addressed specific brands or models in our text. Instead we discuss three broad categories of stunters -- the Delta or Swept-Wing (known as California Style Stunters by almost everyone except Californians), Diamond Wings, and the inflatible stunters which we call Foils.

Before the ink is dry on this page, new kite designs, materials and applications will become available and then commonplace as our infant sport grows and hurries forward into maturity.

I hope and trust that the information contained here will be useful to you who represent Stunt Kiting's future.

But enough of the mushy stuff ... Put this manual in your kite bag and get out to the flying field!

Good Winds!

David Gomberg
March, 1991

CHAPTER ONE:

ALL ABOUT WIND and TERRAIN

WIND CHARACTERISTICS

Most people don't spend a great deal of time thinking about the wind. Sailors, pilots, and other "professionals" may be exceptions, but for ordinary folks, average winds have little effect on their daily lives and go almost unnoticed.

Stunt kite flyers are different.

A kite and the wind together form a system. The wind is the engine. No engine, no flying. For the stunt kite flyer, learning about wind and how to "read" it will make the difference between success and frustration on the flying field.

Experienced flyers have a habit of watching the wind constantly, even when not flying. They watch flags, trees, smoke, ripples on water, and all the other signs of movement in the air. Being aware of the wind is second nature to a proficient flyer. And when the wind is "right", they begin to get a wistful look in their eyes.

One admonishment before we start -- IT'S NEVER THE WIND'S FAULT!!

Many flyers think that the wind should listen to them and do what they tell it to. If it doesn't blow hard enough - or even enough - or soon enough, they get upset with the wind. Be advised -- the wind doesn't care what you think! It does what it wants!

Think of all the energy those flyers wasted being aggravated. Resolve to use that same energy learning to cope with the wind the way it is, and you'll be a much better flyer. You'll soon be able to fly and enjoy yourself in just about any condition. You'll be flying while those others are complaining that the wind doesn't listen!

So ... start watching the wind. Get comfortable with it. Become one of those wistful observers who always notices the breeze.

The wind has two characteristics that concern the stunt kite flyer -- smoothness and strength. We'll talk about **SMOOTHNESS** first.

Finding a smooth, "regular" wind to fly in is important for the same reasons that finding a smooth road to drive on is important. Smooth roads are easier and more pleasant. They cause less wear on your car. Accidents are less likely.

But it is a fact of life that if you want to get where you are going and the only way there is a bumpy road, you'll drive on the bumpy road. There are also people who enjoy going out in a four-wheeler and bouncing off rocks. Kite flying is no different.

Unfortunately, there is no such thing as a "steady breeze" -- just as there's no such thing as a road with no bumps. While it's tempting to think of the wind as a steady, regular progression of air from one point to another, the facts are that it just doesn't happen that way.

Wind suffers many interruptions and indignities. Friction with the ground slows it down; obstacles like trees, buildings, and hills create turbulance; changes in temperature and even the heat of the ground surface affect wind patterns. And, in the face of that, your job as a flyer is to find the smoothest, most regular wind available.

Sound hard? It's not.

Let's look at the wind. We'll represent the wind with arrows. The direction of the arrow indicates the direction of the wind at that point, and the length of the arrow represents wind velocity:

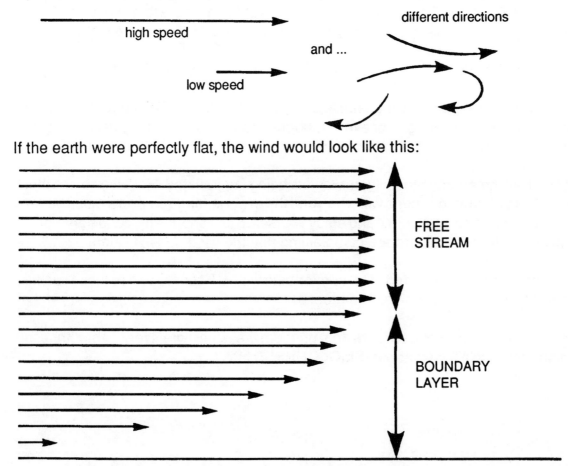

If the earth were perfectly flat, the wind would look like this:

Friction with the ground causes the air near the surface to move more slowly -- even when the wind is quite strong. You can demonstrate this yourself on a windy day simply by lying down on the ground and feeling what it's like down there. Higher up, the wind moves faster, but is still affected by the slower air closer to the ground. This creates a region called the BOUNDARY LAYER -- the region from the ground level up to the level at which the wind is no longer affected. Everything above the Boundary Layer is called the FREE STREAM.

The important things to know about the Boundary Layer are:

> Its thickness varies.
> Its effect on your kite will always be evident at low altitudes (under ten feet).
> Effects will sometimes be apparent at higher levels (up to fifty or sixty feet).

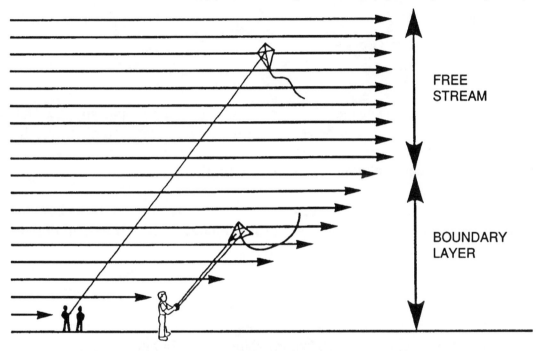

So in some respects, those kids with their $1.25 kite have it better than you do! Their kite will get up into the free stream, while you have to deal with the slower boundary layer. Fortunately, your kite is designed for these conditions and will do just fine. Later on, we'll even talk about how to use the boundary layer to produce some spectacular results.

Wind is caused by uneven atmospheric temperatures. Different temperatures create differences in pressure and, as these imbalances even themselves out, winds result.

Because of differences in land and sea temperatures, an onshore wind can quickly turn into an offshore wind during the early evening. Coping with a relatively sudden turnaround of 90 or more degrees can be challenging to even the most experienced kite flyer.

David Pelham
The Penguin Book of Kites

The boundary layer is something we can't change and which we can actually learn to work with. Turbulence is a different story. Turbulence is definitely bad news.

Turbulence is generated by anything that gets in the wind's way. Even your stunt kite generates some turbulence, but we'll talk about that later.

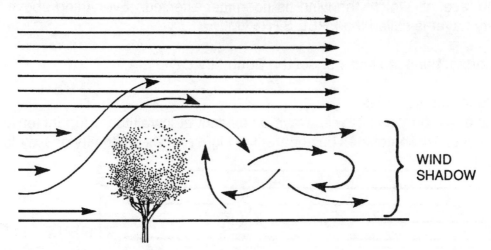

WIND
SHADOW

The turbulent area downwind of an obstacle is called its <u>wind shadow</u>. All wind shadows gradually disappear as you get further away from the obstacle. But not right away. The shadow from a typical tree extends several hundred yards, while a large building can make a shadow a mile long!

The air, flowing over trees, houses and fields, acts much like a river, flowing over rocks, around bends, and through level stretches. Turbulence, in both cases, takes some time to smooth out.

The difficulty with flying in turbulent conditions is that you will experience sudden, irregular, and unpredictable wind shifts. Depending upon the severity of the turbulence, coping with these shifts will range from exhilarating to impossible. So the message is, in short -- If you like crashing, go fly behind a tree.

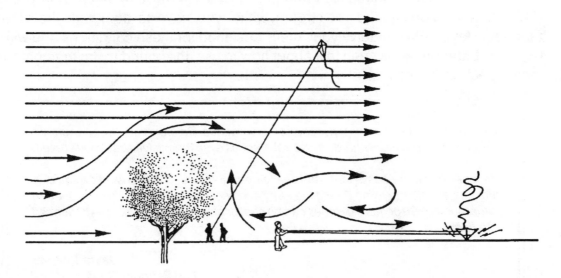

Strength is the other important characteristic of wind.

Since wind is never perfectly smooth, any discussion of wind strength has to refer to its average strength. So when we talk about a "10 mph wind", please understand that the actual wind strength at any instant will vary, but that the "average" will be about ten miles per hour.

Probably the best way to give you a brief overview of wind strength and how it will affect your kite is with the following table. The "Beaufort Scale" was devised by Admiral Sir Frances Beaufort of the British Navy in 1806 as a standard guide for describing the force of wind on sailing ships. (Note the "Beaufort Number" in the left hand column.)

The scale has been modified for land and for kite flyers in particular. We've added a column of information to the scale which describes the effects of the wind on stunt kite flying.

The Beaufort Scale

Beaufort Number and Designation	Average M.P.H.	What to Look For	Effects on Kite Flying
0 Calm	less than 1	No wind; smoke rises vertically.	Stay home and read a good kite book. *
1 Light Air	1-3	Wind direction just shown by smoke.	Visit your local kite store and tell stories about how great the wind was yesterday. *
2 Light Breeze	4-7	Leaves rustle, wind felt on face, flags flap lazily.	Ultra-light kites will fly; use light wind techniques. *
3 Gentle Breeze	8-12	Leaves and small twigs in constant motion; flags extended.	Excellent wind for beginners. Everything flies well with little physical strain.
4 Moderate Breeze	13-18	Raises dust and loose paper; small branches move.	Perfect conditions. The kind of day you can talk about next time there is no wind.
5 Fresh Breeze	19-24	Branches and small trees sway; wavelets form on inland waters.	Flying gets physical; equipment must be in good shape. Use high wind techniques. *
6 Strong Breeze	25-31	Large branches move; whistling in phone and electric wires.	Upper limits for standard stunters. Heavy wind techniques mandatory and reinforced equipment recommended. *
7 Moderate Gale	32-38	Whole trees in motion.	Banzai conditions! Go ski - or stay home and read another good kite book. *

* See special sections on High Wind and Low Wind Flying.

Inexpensive, hand-held wind meters are also available at most kite stores and supply outlets. But remember, they only tell you the wind speed at ground level.

PICKING A FLYING SITE

There are two main things to consider when picking a place to fly: the terrain and site safety.

TERRAIN -- We know from the previous section that it's difficult to fly well in turbulent wind. Turbulence is caused not only by obstacles, but also by the shape of the ground itself. Let's look at the way the wind flows over a hill.

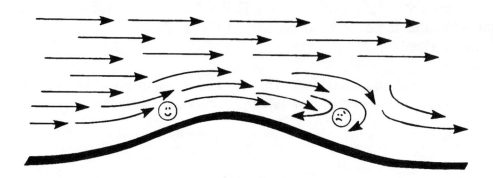

On the windward, or "front" side of a hill, the air flow compresses and speeds up. These are good sites for stunt flying. A hill that's the right shape can even help smooth out some of the turbulence reaching it from farther upwind, cleaning up the flow and making for better flying.

The leeward, or "back" side, however, is different. Wind flowing over the crest of the hill "separates" and causes turbulence that can range from moderate to severe depending on the speed of the wind and the shape of the hill.

> *Chances are that you don't live in an area with perfect flying conditions. So when you do go flying, look for a place which will give you the smoothest, most consistent wind possible.*
>
> *When you fly into turbulent wind, you'll quickly notice an inconsistent pull or jerking on your line and the kite will actually feel like it is "bouncing" along. Hovering will become more difficult and you may suddenly lose control from time to time.*
>
> *If you don't have control, then you probably aren't having fun. Worse yet, you may actually be creating a dangerous situation. The key is to avoid turbulence.*

So if a little slope is good, a steep slope must be better. And that means that a cliff should be a wonderful place to fly, right? Well, not exactly.

The sharp break at the foot of the cliff causes the wind to form a "pocket" of stalled and turbulent air. The break at the top causes turbulence to form just like the back side of a hill. So the general rule is: Stay away from cliffs.

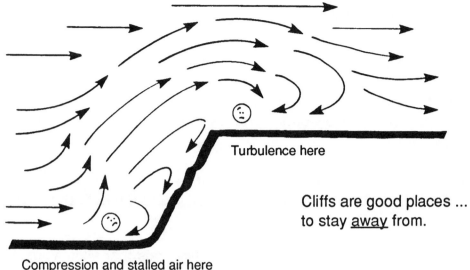

Turbulence here

Cliffs are good places ...
to stay <u>away</u> from.

Compression and stalled air here

The perfect flying site is absolutely flat and has no obstructions for miles in any direction. Those are the kinds of places we travel to for big kite festivals. Unfortunately, most of us have to settle for something a bit closer to home for "regular" flying.

Here's how to make the best of one common situation:

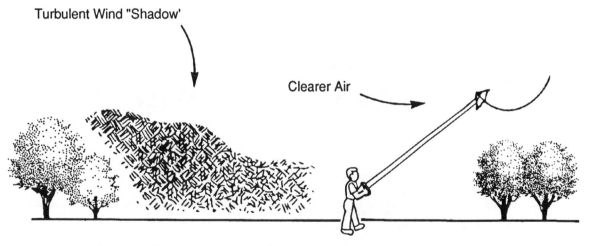

Turbulent Wind "Shadow'

Clearer Air

On a field bounded both upwind and down by obstructions, you're better off flying as close as you safely can to the <u>downwind</u> end of the field. Get as far away as possible from the source of turbulence so the wind will be as "clean" as possible.

> *The basic formula for turbulence is that unsteady winds will extend seven times further than the height of whatever object is causing the disruption. If a tree is 100 feet tall, you need to get 700 feet away to find clean or steady wind.*
>
> *The best advice is to not fly downwind of tall trees, buildings, or geological formations. In fact, whenever possible, avoid flying downwind of any tall obstructions.*

SAFETY and COURTESY

You'll be hearing a lot about safety from us, from your flying friends, from your local shop owner, and from kiteflying organizations. There's a good reason, so pay attention! Any stunt kite you fly is a PROJECTILE -- capable of doing injury and property damage. You can injure others. You can do damage to your surroundings. You can hurt yourself.

Even in a moderate wind, a typical stunt kite can be moving at over 60 miles per hour. **If someone gets hit by anything moving over 60 miles per hour, it's going to hurt!**

Remember, the same rigid fiberglass and graphite rods that allow your kite to handle strong winds and high performance turns are like arrow shafts that puncture people and things. Taut, thin flying lines moving through the air at high speeds are even more dangerous. A wire cheese-cutter uses the same principle.

So unless you enjoy nasty letters from lawyers and insurance companies, BE CAREFUL. Pay close attention to what you're doing just as you would when driving a car, flying a plane, or operating any other potentially hazardous device.

Here's another obvious safety tip: **Stay away from overhead lines.** Anyone who tells you that wet flylines won't conduct electricity hasn't flown in a thunderstorm. Anyone who has flown wet line in a thunderstorm isn't likely to be around to tell you about it!

By the way, dry flylines also conduct electricity. So watch out for power lines. No clouds, no rain ... same result.

And even if you don't get zapped, remember this: The power company carries 13,600 volts on lines less than two feet apart. In 1979, a kite dragged two of those lines together and burned down $15,000,000 worth of Santa Barbara, California.

Most important of all, watch out for people. A typical situation that develops into a hazard looks like this: It's a beautiful day - just you, your kite, and a perfect wind. Soon your aerobatic prowess attracts spectators. Their "oohs" and "aahs" go straight to your head, and soon you're flying "all out".

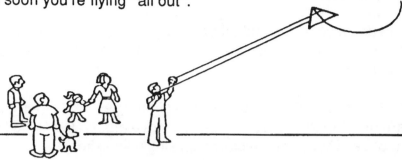

Some children, attracted by the motion and bright color, decide to chase your kite. Your ego tempts you to show off by chasing them back. You dive on them and make them fall down laughing while the crowd applauds. You think everyone is having great fun. The problem is, you may not know it or believe it, but you're in <u>TROUBLE</u>.

Because - no matter how good you are, no matter how good you think you are, you're not good enough...

You turn into an instant jerk...

It doesn't matter that you got away with it the last 100 times, or the last 1,000 times you tried it. It only takes once to hurt someone badly.

Hitting people isn't the only thing to worry about. For the uninformed, a stunt kite can be a scary thing.

The noise your kite makes can frighten people so don't "sneak" up on or "buzz" them. And because flight is more horizontal than verticle, many spectators don't realize how close the kite will be coming. The point here is -- don't just be a safe flyer. Be a considerate and mature flyer as well.

Corey Jensen
Monterey, California

So when you get into a situation like this - and you <u>will</u> -- LAND. Explain the danger to the children and their parents. People will understand. Tell them the best place to watch is up <u>behind</u> the pilot.

Get the area under your kite clear, then resume flying. That way you can put on a dazzling show and be a responsible flyer at the same time. Your spectators will <u>really</u> be impressed.

In Chapter Seven, we talk about how to avoid tangles with other stunt kite flyers. Stunters are mobile, which means they can move around the flying field in order to avoid each other. That's not the case with single line kites.

If you are in an area where "stationary" kites are being flown, watch out for their lines -- especially the ones that are tied down and unattended. Stunt flylines can easily slice through the line used for other kites. Start cutting them down and their owners will come looking for you!

To sum it all up, share the flying space. Be alert. Be careful. Always remember the four "C's" of responsible kiting:

Caution, Courtesy, Common Sense and Control.

Some parks and beaches are now beginning to limit or even prohibit stunt kite flying. This is a direct result of irresponsible flyers who monopolize space or needlessly frighten and injure people. Stunt kites are not dangerous, but some stunt kite flyers are.

For these reasons, liability insurance has become a major issue for kite clubs and groups sponsoring stunt kite events. These new expenses may actually force the cancellation of some contests.

The most important thing that stunt kite enthusiasts can do to ensure the future of the sport is concentrate on safety and courtesy.

CHAPTER TWO:

FIRST FLIGHT

BEFORE YOU LEAVE THE HOUSE

Most people who ride bikes remember falling off or crashing when they first started learning. So did they quit trying? Of course not -- they picked themselves up and kept on practicing.

Keep that in mind when you first start flying your stunter. Crashing isn't a requirement -- but it is likely to occur. That said, let's go flying! If you've never flown before and there's no one around to teach you, here are some things to help you get off the ground.

1. Almost every stunt kite on the market comes with an instruction sheet. If you have one, read it. If you didn't get one, contact the store or manufacturer where you bought the kite and get one.

Instruction sheets usually contain specific information on assembly, fine tuning, replacement parts, and warranties. This is important stuff! Put the sheet someplace where you can find it later. You may want to take it with you on a first flight to help with assembly, but don't lose it.

2. Have you read the section on picking a flying site? It helps to know where you are going before you try to go there.

3. Check the wind. For your first few flying sessions it should be blowing 8-12 m.p.h. Less or more is all right, but not as easy.

4. Take a helper if at all possible. Having a "ground crew" eases the process considerably. If no help is available, be sure to read the section about Self Launching and take along a piece of scrap dowel, or a screwdriver to use as a ground anchor. We'll explain more about anchors later. Also, remember to take your kite, any stray parts, your flylines, and some handles.

We only mention this because we're good at forgetting stuff like that.

KITE ASSEMBLY

Assembly is simply a matter of following the instructions provided by the manufacturer. Each kite is somewhat different, but there are a few common things to watch out for.

Nearly all stunt kites use clear vinyl tubing to connect cross-struts to the kite. Some have the tubing in the nose-piece, some use additional support-struts to withstand the compression stresses that are encountered in flight.

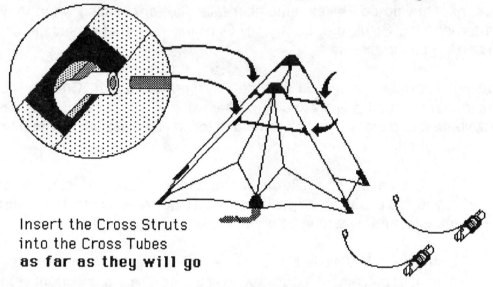

Insert the Cross Struts
into the Cross Tubes
as far as they will go

Insert the struts into the vinyl tubes as far as they will go. Use a steady, even pressure when you push the strut in and don't force anything.

If you don't push the struts all the way in, the kite may not handle smoothly. Also, when you crash (and eventually, you will), the struts will have a tendency to pop out unless they are properly inserted.

> *Sometimes struts are too loose. Carry a roll of electrician's tape to "enlarge" loose spars.*
>
> *When removing spars - "twist" while pulling. It will save your hands. In conditions of high humidity, spars may need to removed later since nothing short of a world class wrestler can pry them loose. To make the job easier, try putting some common baby or talcum powder on the struts first. Don't use oil or other lubricants since they dry sticky .*
>
> **Cris Batdorff**
> **Manistee, Michigan**

When you have all the struts attached, take a close look at your bridle lines. Check them all and make sure none are wrapped around or under one of the struts. This is the easiest mistake to make in the excitment of preparing for a first launch. Believe us, overlook this bridle-check and the excitement is just beginning!

Tangled lines mean crashing kites ...

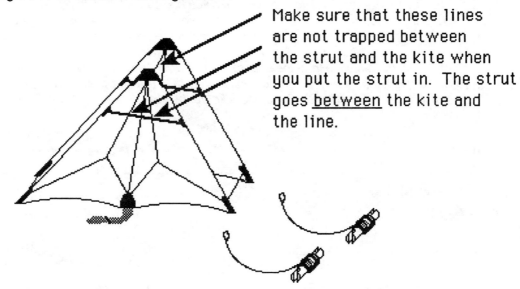

Make sure that these lines are not trapped between the strut and the kite when you put the strut in. The strut goes <u>between</u> the kite and the line.

Next, attach your flylines.

If your lines don't already have a loop or swivel at the ends, read the discussion on knots in the Flylines Chapter. Swivels aren't essential but they do help reduce line twisting and tangles. The strongest connections are made by attaching lines directly to the scissor-clips or snap swivels installed on most kites.

Open the clip and connect the loop at the end of the flyline using a "larkshead" knot. This method will reduce strain on the line, prevent slippage, and keep the line from "sawing" constantly against the metal clip.

Finally, notice that many line and handle sets are color coded red and black. The red handle goes on the right side of the kite. Remember, red - right! That way you can get the handles in the correct hands every time and avoid the embarrasing condition known as "WRONG HANDITIS". It helps to mark the line at both ends too so you can attach it properly to the kite or handles.

Most stunt kites are pre-assembled at the factory so that you can spend your time flying instead of assembling. Only a few quick connections are required.

Putting your stunt kite together and getting it ready for its first flight should take about the same time, or less, as reading these assembly directions.

LAYOUT

Unroll the flylines directly upwind.

Your lines should be between 100 and 150 feet long. Shorter lines reduce response time and make the kite move too fast for most inexperienced flyers. Longer lines make maneuvers hard to complete unless you have _very_ long arms.

Line of 100 to 150 feet maximize responsiveness within the "flight envelope". We'll discuss the flight envelope in much more detail later. For now, take our word for it and USE AT LEAST ONE-HUNDRED FEET of line.

After you have unrolled the lines, check them carefully to make sure they're the same length. Commercially packaged lines are seldom cut to _exactly_ identical lengths, so take some time and save yourself some trouble later.

If the difference is more than four inches, re-tie the loop at the kite end of the longer line to make it shorter. Smaller changes can be made where you attach the lines to the handles, but ideally, THE LINES SHOULD BE EXACTLY EQUAL.

Adjust the lines until they are as close to exactly the same length as you can get them. This is also a good time to make sure the lines are securely fastened to your handles.

LAUNCHING

ASSISTED LAUNCHING -- Here's how it works if you have a helper.

Pick up the handles. If they are color-coded, make sure the RED one is in your RIGHT hand.

Have your helper pick up the kite from behind, and hold it by the base and center struts. (If you are flying more than one kite, they should hold the last one in the stack.) Keep a little tension between the two of you so that the flylines are off the ground.

From your helper's viewpoint, the launch should look like this:

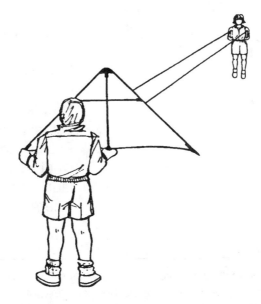

Now complete the "Pre-launch Checklist". Do <u>everything</u> on this list before every launch.

Pre-launch Checklist

1. Check the area under where your kite will be flying for possible hazards - mainly people.

2. Look behind you to make sure that you have a clear path if you need to back up. Backing up is a legitimate and natural way of helping your kite out of trouble, but it can get <u>you</u> into trouble. (We once forgot this second pre-launch step and backed into a smelly drainage ditch!)

3. Make sure your flylines have equal tension so that your kite will launch straight.

4. If there are other kite flyers around, check the sky for traffic. When it is clear, announce to any nearby pilots that you are ready to launch.

Finished with the checklist? On your signal, your helper should give the kite a gentle upward push, then let go. There is no need to be forceful. Just toss it.

> *It's not unusual for new fliers to crash a few times when they first practice launching. That's fine -- as long as you don't hit anyone on the way down.*
>
> *Your kite and all of your line should be layed out before you launch. Look around to make sure that there are no obstacles or people anywhere within reach of your lines. This is the only way to know that you are clear and safe.*

And guess what?

YOU'RE FLYING!!

Now we sincerely hope that, before you actually launch your kite, you read the Piloting Basics section, which deals with what to do immediately after you've launched. If not, go collect your kite from wherever it ended up, and read it now.

> After the launch, your helper should _quickly_ move downwind and away from the sweep of the kite. Often, helpers become "mesmerized" by the kite's flight. They forget to move and can be seriously hurt by a sudden loop or crash.
>
> The best way to "keep" a helper is to keep them from getting hurt!

SELF LAUNCHING -- Now here's how it works if you're by yourself.

Self Launching is not difficult, but it helps to have at least a few flights in your logbook before you try it. The main thing that a helper does is give you a straight "boost" through the Boundary Layer that we talked about earlier. Doing it by yourself takes a little practice so expect to have to try it as many as three or four times to get it right. After that, it's easy.

Self launching is also slightly different depending on whether you are flying a "Delta" or "Swept-Wing" kite (also called "California Style" stunters since that's where many first came from), a "Foil", or one of the "Diamond Wing" kites.

We'll start by explaining how to self launch Deltas and Diamonds.

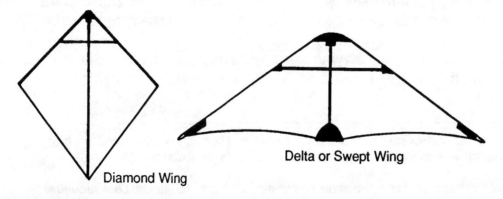

Diamond Wing

Delta or Swept Wing

DELTAS and DIAMONDS: Stunters come in lots of shapes and sizes, but generally speaking, on Diamond Wings, the center strut is longest. On Deltas wings, the side struts are the longest part of the kite.

16

1.   After you unroll the lines upwind, "stake" your handles down. Remember that anchor we talked about earlier? Here's what it it's for:

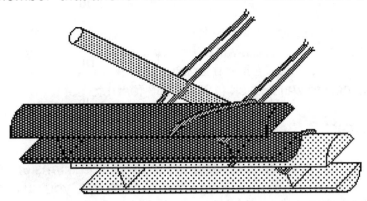

Stick it in the ground at an angle away from the kite. Hook the loops in the lines or your handles over it.

2. Walk back to the kite and stand it up using the flylines as a tension against the wind. Be sure that the kite isn't standing straight up when you're done. Unless it leans away from the handles a little, it will try to take off and fly by itself!

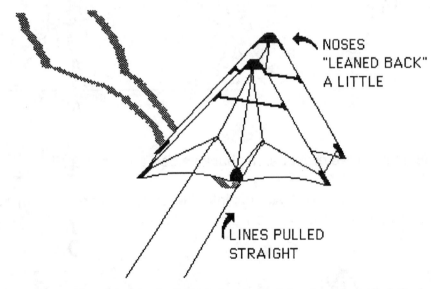

NOSES
"LEANED BACK"
A LITTLE

LINES PULLED
STRAIGHT

Delta stunters should stand on their base and be leaning slightly back. Diamond Wing kites should be standing on a side strut with the nose pointed at an angle into the ground.

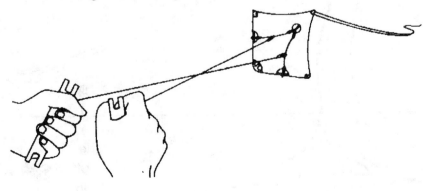

3. Now go back to the handles and carefully pick them up. (Pick up your stake too since you'll need it for your next launch.) Try not to let the kite move.

It's okay for the kite to tilt a little farther back while you pick up the handles, but if you pull it toward you it will either try to take-off prematurely, or just fall over on its face. Similarly, if you let it lean back too far, the kite will fall over and you'll need to walk back (100 to 150 feet!) to set it up again.

4. Don't forget the Pre-Launch Checklist.

5. For Delta Wing kites, you will need to keep equal tension on both lines during the launch. Diamond Wing kites require that you pull up a bit on the line attached to the SKYWARD side strut during the launch. Got it?

Now, just take three or four steps backwards - and you're off!

Your Delta Wing should lift straight into the air. A Diamond Stunter or stack will roll over and turn skyward. Then it too will take off.

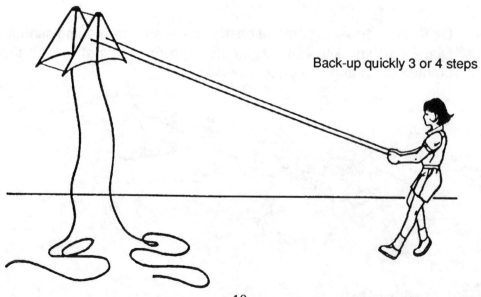

Back-up quickly 3 or 4 steps

Many flyers will stake out a kite ready to launch, and then walk away and leave the kite unattended. It's almost too obvious to mention, but, because the practice is so common, we'll say it anyway: Leaving your kite staked out and unattended is a DUMB IDEA! A hundred feet of line, strung out a few inches above the ground, is an accident waiting to happen. Don't do it!

Self Launching Foils:

"Ram Air Inflated Airfoils" (we call them "Foils") are clearly distinct from other types of stunters. Most have only one spar and no bridles at all. And they certainly won't "lean back" against the flylines ready to launch. Stake out a Foil on the ground with tension on the line, and the kite will launch itself!

There are two important things to remember about launching and flying Foils:

A Foil will only fly when it is right side up. The right side is the "rounded side". Usually, when not being flown, a Foil is left in an upside-down or inverted position to prevent unintentional launches.

A Foil will only fly when the cells are inflated by the wind. Try facing it into the wind, and shaking it lightly to "open" it up. Make sure there is no sand or debris in any of the cells.

In an assisted launch, your helper should stand behind or beside the kite and hold it by the spar. Holding the leading edge or trailing edge will prevent the Foil's cells from being properly inflated by the wind. Make sure the cells are inflated and the lines are taut before releasing.

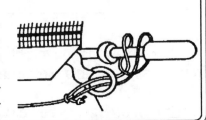

Self Launches for Foils aren't difficult but they do take some practice.

1. Lay the kite out on the ground, right side-up, with the leading or front edge facing into the wind. Then unroll your flylines upwind. Be careful that the kite doesn't try to launch by itself in stronger winds.

2. Remember your Pre-Launch Checklist.

3. Place equal tension on both lines and take three or four steps backward. The Foil will lift into the air and gain speed as the cells inflate and the kite arcs or "flexes".

Launching in heavier winds may actually be more difficult because the kite will begin to lift-off before you can get to the handles and control the launch.

The trick here is to lay the Foil out upside-down. Cross your lines so the Right Handle is on the Right Side. Now pull sharply on one line. Pull it across the other. The kite should swivel around and flip over, right side up. The cells will inflate, the kite will quickly rise into the wind, and you'll be real impressed with yourself.

Pulling the kite across rough or rocky ground will damage the sail. Pulling it across the beach will force some sand into the cells and throw the Foil off balance. If you don't get a lift-off almost at once, STOP PULLING.

A number of new maneuverable Airfoils are now being designed and becoming commercially available. Some have no spars. Others have very complex bridles.

No matter what type or size Foil you fly, the basics of launching remain the same.

CHAPTER THREE: PILOTING BASICS

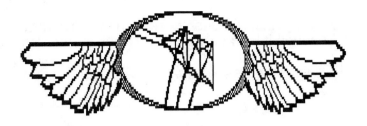

STEERING

All right! Now let's fly. Here's how to steer:

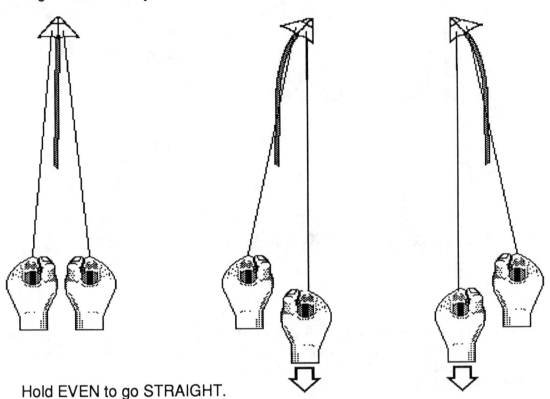

Hold EVEN to go STRAIGHT.

PULL RIGHT to turn RIGHT.

PULL LEFT to turn LEFT.

And that's all there is to it! There are three and only three basic steering movements. Any maneuver you do, from the simplest to the most complex, will just be a combination of Left Turns, Right Turns, and Straight Lines.

> *If your lines are the same length and your kite is properly tuned, the kite will respond as shown. If one line is shorter and you hold your handles together, the kite thinks you're puling on the shorter line.*
>
> **Corey Jensen**
> **Monterey, California**

Now let's talk about each of these basic steering movements.

21

STRAIGHT doesn't necessarily mean straight UP. Your kite is flying "straight" when it is traveling in a straight line across the sky IN ANY DIRECTION.

These kites are all flying STRAIGHT.

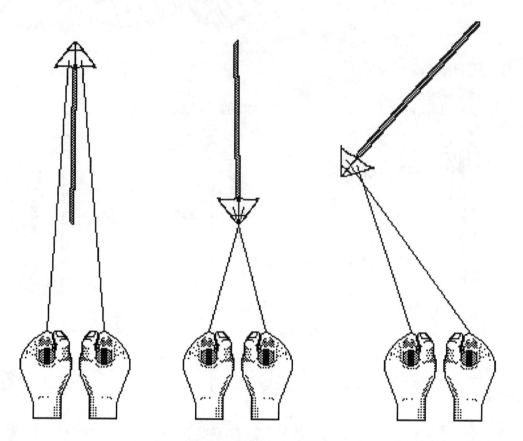

It's a common misconception among new flyers that, when they bring the lines even, the kite will go up. It won't. Just as a car has no natural inclination to go North, a stunt kite has no natural tendency to go in any particular direction. It does what you tell it to.

> *Some types of stunt kites are better for certain types of flying than others. Certain models are superior for flying straight, turning sharp corners, doing loops, pulling tails, or going fast. Similarly, some are better in different types of wind than others.*
>
> *This isn't just a question of whether you are flying a Delta Wing, Diamond, or Foil. Some Deltas perform certain maneuvers better than other Deltas.*
>
> *The best thing you can do is experiment with different types and brands of kites.*
>
> *Some stores allow customers to "test fly" products. Some flyers let people "try out" their kites (although it's sometimes asking a lot to let a stranger experiment with your expensive stunter). If all else fails, try watching other kites and comparing how they behave under different conditions.*

Now about turns ... When you pull with your right hand, the kite turns to its right. Notice that it doesn't necessarily go towards the right side of the sky.

In each of these illustrations, the kite is turning to its right. Left turns work exactly the same way.

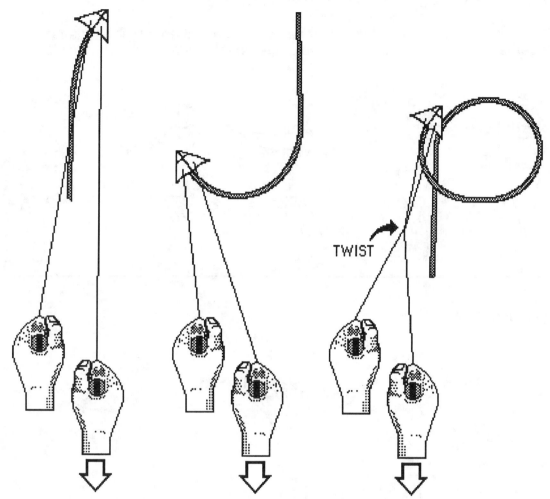

TWIST

In one figure, the flyer has held right while the kite completed a full circle and the lines have twisted over each other. There are three things to remember about twisted lines:

1. As far as the kite is concerned, it has just done a "right turn". Nothing unusual has happened.

2. As far as you are concerned, the fact that the lines have twisted has ABSOLUTELY NO EFFECT on the way the kite now flies. Right is still right. Left is still left. You can keep right on flying.

3. To get rid of the twists -- just turn the other direction! The important thing to try and keep track of is which way you turned to get the twist in the first place. It also helps to remember how many twists you put in the line.

Your head may have a little trouble with this at first, but it soon goes away.

You can easily fly with as many as 5 or 10 twists in the line and the kite will still control just fine. If you make several turns and find that "resistance" is starting to build up on the line, don't worry. The kite is just trying to tell you that, maybe, you should start turning the other way ...

BODY POSITIONS

You can make flying easier on yourself if you relax.

Keep your arms at your sides, your elbows tucked in, and your hands fairly close together. And keep your eyes on your kite. In other words, **fly like THIS**:

NOT like this:

Remember, the kite only recognizes PULL LEFT, PULL RIGHT, and FLY STRAIGHT. Everything else is wasted energy.

    Holding your arms higher doesn't make the kite go up!
    Squeezing the handles tighter doesn't increase control!
    Moving your hips doesn't move the kite!
    Holding your hands farther apart makes control more difficult!
    Waving your arms makes them tired quicker!
    Jerking on the lines will make the kite go faster -- and probably crash harder!

Focus on your flying. Keep your movements smooth and your arms under control. Any extra effort won't improve your flying and will only attract more attention.

In future sections about advanced flying techniques, we'll talk about how to use your arms and body to enhance your flying. For now <u>relax</u>, keep your arms by your sides, and let the kite do the flying while you just steer.

And remember to smile a little! This is supposed to be fun!

FIRST MANEUVER

Let's go back to the moment just after you've launched, and do your first maneuver. Master this one flying sequence, and you'll be well on your way to becoming an accomplished stunt kite pilot.

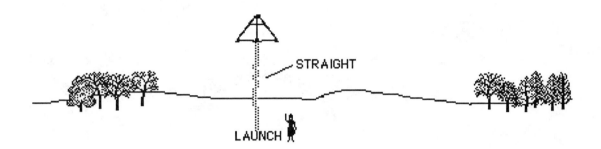

Immediately after launch, fly the kite straight up. You'll be holding the flylines at equal tension. If the kite veers to one side, add a little tension to the opposite line.

      If the kite veers LEFT, pull a little RIGHT.
      If it veers RIGHT, pull a little LEFT.

Let the kite fly up 30 or 40 feet, to an angle of 30 degrees or so. Don't let it fly up too high just yet. The higher it goes, the slower it goes, and right now you want speed and maneuverability.

When it reaches a comfortable altitude, PULL RIGHT.

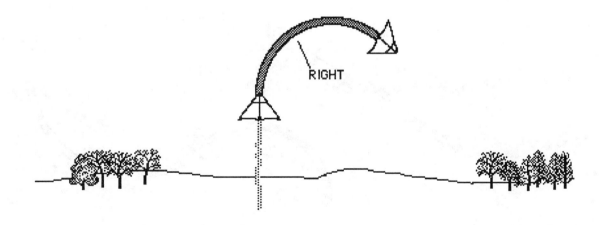

The kite will turn right. You don't have to pull very hard or very far. Pull gently and the kite will enter a nice, comfortable turn. Let it turn until it has just passed horizontal.

25

Then . . . . PULL LEFT.

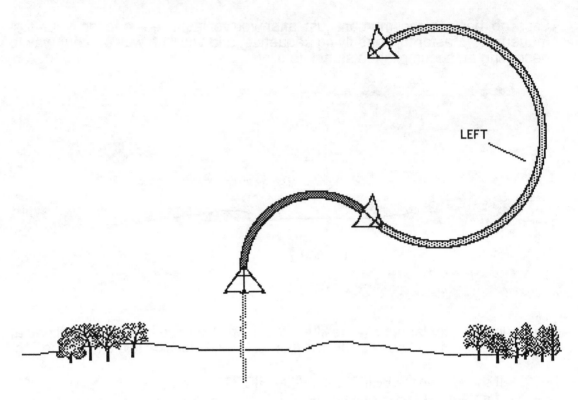

PULL GENTLY, and the kite will enter a left turn. Let it turn until it has gone all the way around to just past horizontal again.

Then .... GO STRAIGHT.

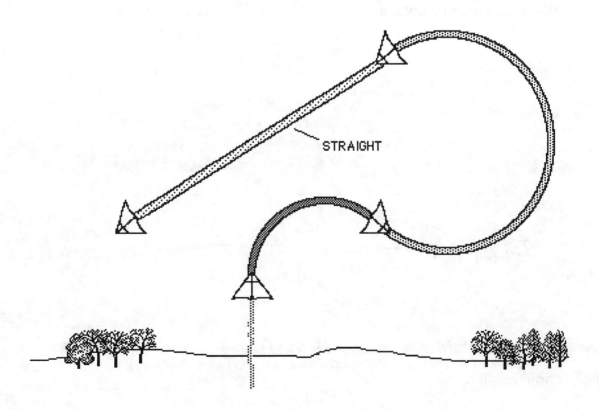

26

Now .... PULL RIGHT again.

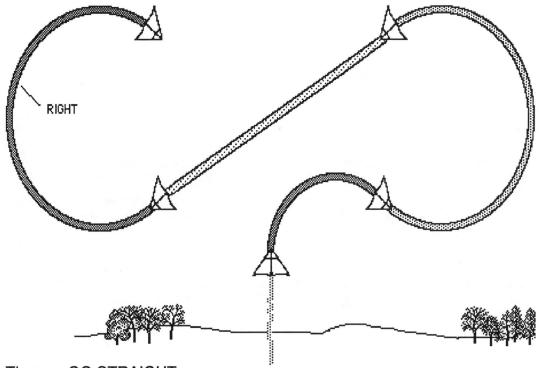

RIGHT

Then .... GO STRAIGHT.

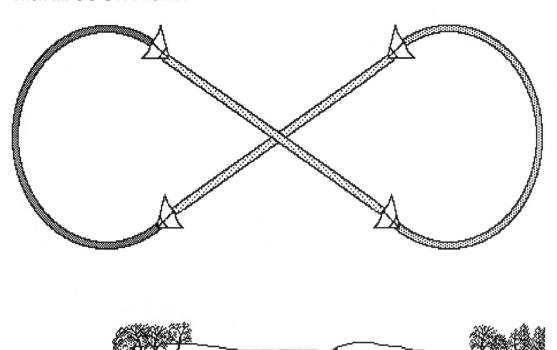

CONGRATULATIONS!! You've just done a <u>horizontal figure eight</u>. Now do it again.

Pull left, straight, pull right, straight.
Left, straight, right, straight.

Notice that what you're doing with your hands "feels" like "left, right, left, right ..." instead of "left, straight, right, straight...". That's perfectly normal. We'll come across other cases where what you "feel" is different from what you're actually doing as we get deeper into the flying process.

The quickest way to get comfortable with flying a stunt kite is to fly horizontal eights over and over, testing the control response and the reaction of the kite to the wind.

Try making your turns bigger and smaller. The harder you pull, the tighter the turn, up to a point. Your kite reacts just like a car. If you try to turn too tightly at too high a speed, you'll skid. Try pulling hard, and watch what happens.

We'll be telling you over and over that the best flying techniques are **finesse, precision,** and **delicacy of control** rather than brute force. Racing drivers don't force the issue. Neither do expert stunt kiters.

Try flying farther out to the left and right. Notice that, as the kite gets farther out to the side, it loses drive and goes slower. For now, be sure to turn back towards the center before the kite loses too much speed. We'll talk about what to do out at the edges of your flight envelope later.

SECOND MANEUVER

Have you done lots of horizontal eights? Had your kite airborne for five minutes at a time without a crash? Great! Let's do a loop.

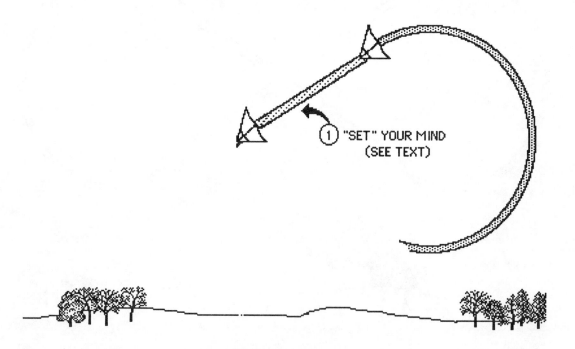

Loops are easy to do. But sometimes, the first few times, a new flyer will unconsciously bring their hands together as soon as the kite points at the ground. This is a holdover from the common thought that holding the lines even makes the kite "go up". It results in a crash.

To avoid that problem, start when the kite is in the position shown. Concentrate on your hands, and "set" your mind with the thought that you are going to PULL RIGHT and HOLD RIGHT NO MATTER WHAT.

Then do it ...

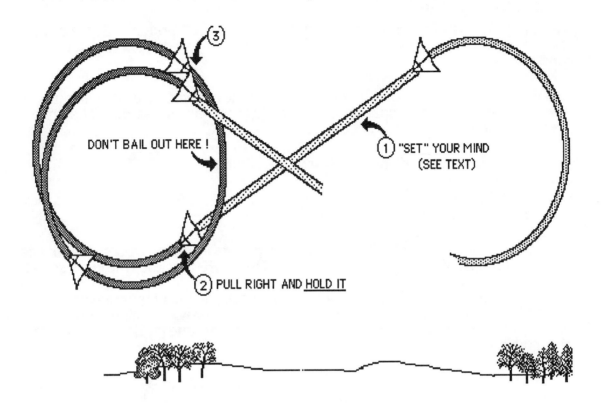

Your heart may be in your throat when the kite points straight down. (That's why the drawing says, "DON'T BAIL OUT HERE!")

Keep thinking PULL RIGHT and put this picture in your mind:

Hold right until the kite flies all the way around to the point labelled 3. Then resume your normal horizontal eights.

Wasn't so bad, was it?

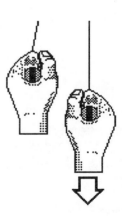

Remember, the fact that the lines are now twisted over each other means <u>nothing at all</u> as far as controlling the kite is concerned. It will fly and steer exactly the same.

Continue those horizontal eights until you're ready, then try a loop the other direction. Everything will work the same. You'll PULL LEFT and hold it until the kite flies all the way around. And the lines will untwist!

LANDING

There are three kinds of stunt kite landings: Accidental, Normal, and something we call "The Eagle Has Landed". The "Eagle" is one of the more difficult maneuvers you'll do, and requires a fair amount of skill and practice. We'll save talking about it for the Advanced Techniques section, and concentrate of the first two types here.

ACCIDENTAL LANDINGS -- Accidental landings WILL happen. (Some people insist on calling them "crashes") We like to say that, "If you don't crash, you're not trying hard enough!"

Follow proper procedures, and crashing is not likely to hurt your kite or anything else. At worst, you may break a spar or strut which is fairly easy to replace. The impact on your ego is usually the worst part.

Here are a few tips that will minimize any real damage:

1. Make sure, as part of your Pre-launch Checklist, that you aren't flying over anything that's _living_, _expensive_, or _tall_.

2. If you find yourself in trouble, and the ground is getting closer, or your kite is in danger of hitting someone, MOVE FORWARD to reduce the kite's speed.

Your normal reaction in a crash situation will be to hold the handles tighter and to pull back on them to try to save the situation. That is exactly the _wrong_ thing to do. Pulling the handles will cause the kite to accelerate and hit the ground _harder_ than if you had done nothing. Like this:

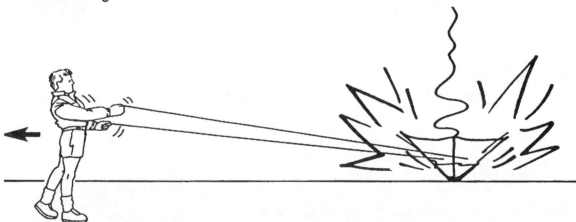

A stunt kite depends on line tension to fly. No tension -- no flying. If you let go, your kite will stop almost instantly in midair and then float down like a leaf. It will not "fly away" like a traditional kite, because without line tension it has no aerodynamic ability at all.

> Never throw your handles in the air, and try not to lose them both. Without your handles, you have no control at all. If you are flying a strong pulling kite, or if the wind is blowing hard, RUN toward the kite to reduce its speed or avoid an accident.
>
> Some stunt kites - particularly the Foil designs - are capable of going a long way on their own if you release both handles. The drag of the lines or handles may provide enough line tension to keep the kite airborne. You can damage those expensive lines. And remember, flying handles can be _dangerous_!

30

If you have time, reduce line tension by walking quickly or running towards the kite. Moving toward the kite reduces speed and lets things happen gently without the possibility of tangling the kite up. It's the <u>SAFEST</u>, <u>SUREST WAY</u> to save a potentially bad situation!

You may still hit something or someone, but at least you won't hit them hard.

If one flyline breaks in mid-flight, the kite will receive the message that one line is being pulled hard and the other has gone slack. The result is a series of <u>uncontrolled</u>, very tight loops that are both dangerous and a bit frightening.

Hang on for a moment to keep the kite airborne, warn people as loudly as you can, and then bring the kite down by letting go or running toward it. This will bring the kite down fast and soft, and limit line twists.

Running toward the kite gives you maximum control in a bad situation.

NORMAL LANDINGS -- A normal, planned landing takes advantage of the fact that, as the kite flies farther "out" to the right or left, it loses drive and speed. A landing is, simply, flying the kite to the point where it runs out of forward drive at the same time it reaches the ground.

Here's how it works ... We've shown a landing to the right, but you can land to either side:

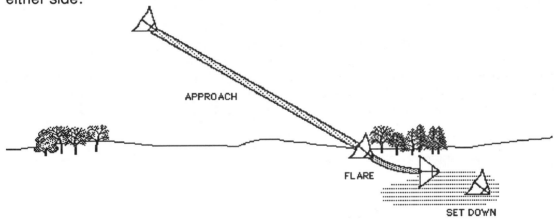

APPROACH - Start from medium altitude, to the left of center. Fly down towards the ground at a shallow angle, as shown. This will take your kite out to the right.

FLARE - When the kite reaches an altitude of four feet or so, make a gentle left turn or "flare". This will bring the kite parallel to the ground. When the kite turns horizontal, it should be about a foot above the ground. If you are far enough to the right, the kite will be just barely moving.

SET DOWN - The kite should practically land itself now. Make a very gentle RIGHT turn, and the kite will settle onto the ground. For the gentlest possible landing, touch the wingtip to the ground, and the kite will settle gracefully onto its nose.

Landing complete ...

BETTER NORMAL LANDINGS -- After you've done a few successful Normal Landings, try this:

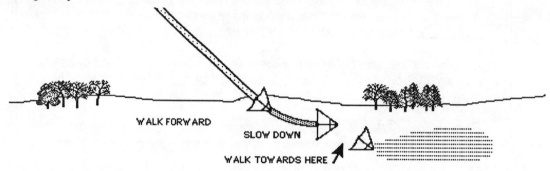

WALK FORWARD

SLOW DOWN

WALK TOWARDS HERE

As you start your Approach, begin walking towards the point where the kite will land. When the kite enters the Boundary Layer, and it's time to flare, slow down, but keep walking.

To set down, just take a couple of steps forward at your normal rate. The kite will set down like a feather. Easier, isn't it?

What you've just done is also a good exercise in <u>throttle control</u>. You have SUBTRACTED your walking speed from the wind speed -- allowing better control over your landing approach and the transition into the Boundary Layer. When you ran toward the kite to avoid an accident, you were using throttle control to reduce the kite's speed. This is just like cutting the throttle on an airplane to land!

You'll find that, with practice, you can pick your landing spot anywhere within a wide area, and set down precisely on it.

Never clean your stunt kite with anything stronger than water! Strong solvents will remove the nylon coating and make the sail more porous.

OOPS! Already ruined your kite by cleaning it with a commercial solvent? Spray the skin with Scotchguard. It will coat the fabric and help save the ruined kite. This is not a permanent method, but it will save or rejuvenate old, windworn sails.

Al Hargus III
Chicago, Illinois

PACKING UP

When you're finished flying for the day, take a few minutes to pack your kite properly. It will help prevent damage to the kite, and will save you a lot of grief the next time you go out to fly.

The first thing to do is land. It will help a lot if the lines are not crossed, so take the time to untwist while you are still in the air.

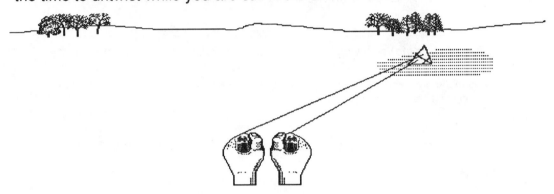

Put the handles down right where you are. Don't take them with you, or you'll be untangling flyline for a week! <u>Disconnect the lines from the kite</u>. Put the ends of the lines down where they are, and leave the lines stretched out on the field for now.

If you're flying a single Delta or "Swept Wing" kite, remove all the spreader struts from their vinyl or metal retaining tubes. Fold the kite <u>carefully</u>, making certain not to wrap the fabric around any metal fittings. Put the kite and all the spars away in their bag where they won't get lost.

NOW, wind up your flylines. Incidentally, this is a good time to check your lines to make sure they are still the same length. After several hours of heavy flying, some flylines may stretch. If you measure them now, you'll be ready to start right in when you set-up next time.

DON'T wind both lines onto one handle in a way that will twist the lines around each other. Otherwise, you'll find all those twists still there the next time you take the lines out.

DON'T walk towards the far end of the line as you wind it up! Let it drag towards you while you stand in one place. That way, any twist in the line will have a chance to work itself out while you wind.

Besides being a mess to untangle, one other reason you don't want to twist the lines is that twisted lines stretch more, slowing control response.

The best approach at first is to wind up the lines one at a time. Then pick up any stray stuff you may have left on the flying field -- and you're done until next time.

> *Tired of wrapping your flying lines up one at a time? Wrap them both on the same handle or winder ... just make sure that the lines wrap and unwrap from the same side of the handle or spool. If you unwrap from the wrong side, you will suffer the "curse of a million wraps"!*
>
> **Lee Sedgwick**
> **Erie, Pennsylvania**

REPAIRS

Accidents occasionally happen. And unfortunately, those accidents sometimes result in punctures or tears in the stunter's sails, or in broken spars.

The best material for repairing nylon sails is ripstop nylon tape. Made of the same material as your kite, it is available in many kite supply outlets and comes in a variety of colors. Buy a few pieces that match your kite's colors and have them ready for when that accident happens. You can make quick repairs and go right on flying.

Replacement spars can also be bought from kite stores or manufacturers. Again, it helps to have a few on hand for when the inevitable happens. Remember to use the same type of spar, and particularly, the same weight, thickness, and length as the original.

> *A note on relative durability... If your kite rips - you can't fly. If your line breaks - you can't fly. If you spar breaks, you can insert a new spar.*
>
> *Spar replacement is the least expensive way to absorb stress without long term damage. As in life, you can ignore stress but it doesn't go away. Spars bend and recover. Nylon just stretches out of shape.*
>
> **Corey Jensen**
> **Monterey, California**

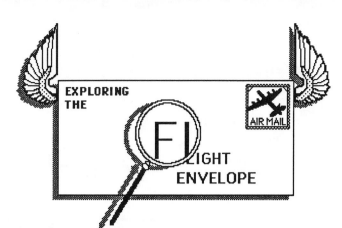

CHAPTER FOUR:

EXPLORING the FLIGHT ENVELOPE

So what's a flight envelope? It's all the conditions under which a flying machine will fly. The conditions for an airplane include speed, altitude, throttle setting, weight, angle of attack, and many more. For a kite, the wind speed, tuning, line tension, control position, and so on are the conditions that allow flight. Think of the envelope as just that -- an envelope. Inside the envelope are all the conditions that allow flight. Outside the envelope is everything else.

If you're "inside the flight envelope", you're flying. If you're "outside the envelope", you're not.

A rock doesn't fly (not enough lift).
An airplane in a stall doesn't fly (not enough speed, too much angle).
A kite in too little wind doesn't fly (not enough power).

Inside the envelope there are many things to explore. In this section, we will look at the way the kite reacts to the wind, and the ways you can expect it to act under various conditions

Let's take a look at the wind from a new perspective:

When you fly, your kite is generally downwind. Sort of. But as you already know, it flies over a large area, and the wind affects the kite differently depending upon where it is in that area and which direction it's traveling.

Here's a new picture of your flying area:

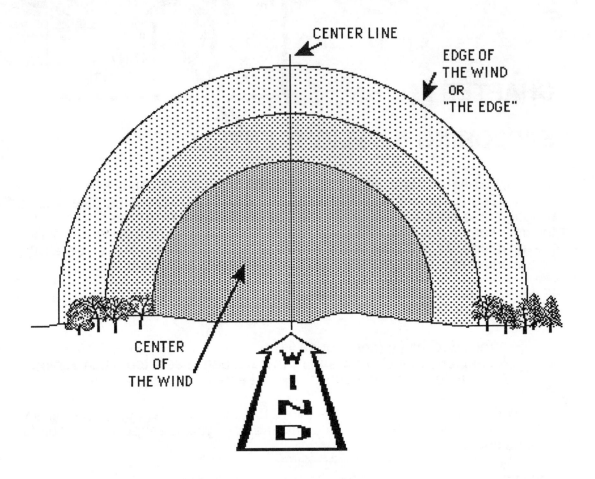

The CENTER LINE is an imaginary vertical line <u>directly</u> downwind. It's a handy reference, and something to keep in your mind as you fly.

The CENTER OF THE WIND is the area in which the kite has good speed and maneuverability. You did your first maneuvers in the Center. The size of this area is not fixed, but varies depending on the strength of the wind, the state of the kite's tuning, and sometimes on local conditions. You'll soon learn the "feel" of the Center, and know when it grows and shrinks.

The EDGE OF THE WIND is the imaginary line in the sky that represents the farthest "out" to the left or right the kite will fly. Any time the kite is at the Edge, it has no forward drive. It will still fly, it just won't go anywhere. This condition is called a hover. We'll talk about hovering shortly. It's difficult to force the kite beyond the Edge. If you do, the kite will still be in the air, but it will be outside its flight envelope and <u>not</u> really flying.

Between the Center and the Edge, the kite will fly fine, but slower than in the Center. Its response to controls will be somewhat different than in the Center, too. The kite will have the characteristics you already know, combined with those we're going to talk about now.

Incidentally, it is helpful to remember that everything in the flying area grows and shrinks in proportion depending on the strength of the wind. In strong wind, the kite will fly over an angle of 120 degrees or more. In light wind, the angle shrinks to as little as 45 degrees or even less. In all cases, the proportions of the various parts remain the same.

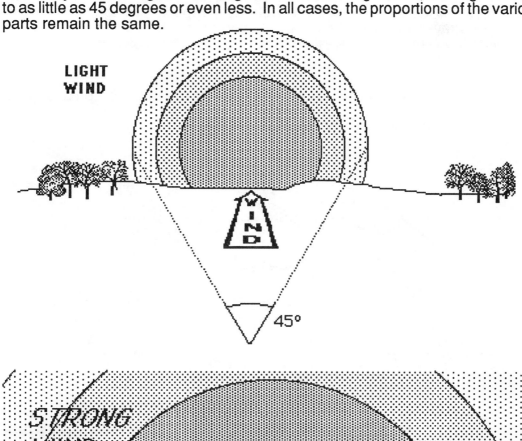

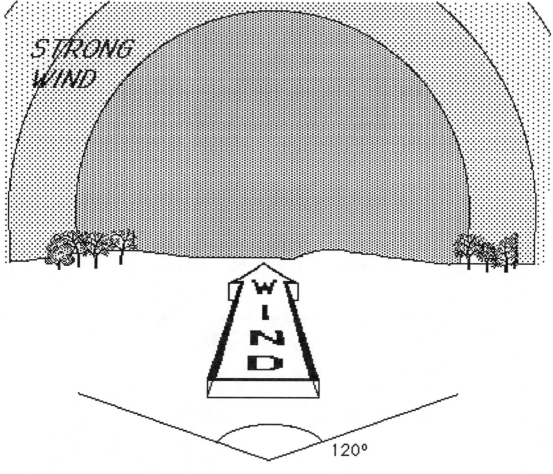

CONTROL RESPONSE AT THE EDGE

While doing beginning maneuvers, you stayed in the Center of the Wind. Steering was fairly straightforward. Pull left to turn left; pull right to turn right. If the kite strayed out towards the Edge, you probably brought it back quickly towards the Center. Now we'll go to the Edge deliberately, and take a look at what happens there.

(NOTE: It's much easier to do this the first time if the wind is 8 mph or stronger.)

Point the kite STRAIGHT UP. Hold your hands STILL and WAIT.

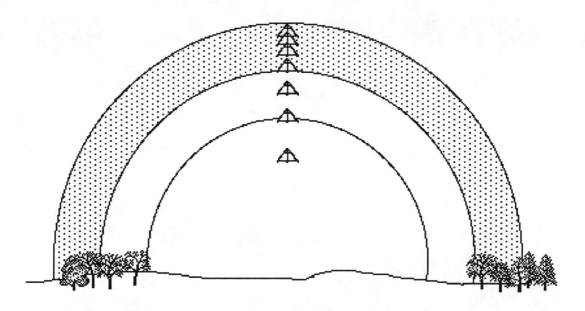

The kite will fly up, slow down, and stop! It's still flying. As a matter of fact, as far as the kite's concerned, it's still flying <u>in a straight line</u>. It doesn't know it's not going anywhere. This position is called a **HOVER**.

One very important thing has changed, however. The line pull has almost completely disappeared. There should only be as much line pull as the physical weight of the kite.

Hover for a little while, and notice the other important thing about flying near the Edge: YOUR CONTROL MOVEMENTS ARE <u>MUCH</u> SMALLER AND MORE SUBTLE.

If the kite starts to drift, just an ounce or two of pull will guide it back. Experiment with this, applying more, then less pull to turn the kite back and forth across the top of the sky.

Now turn out of the hover.

Use a <u>small</u> control movement:

The kite will turn gracefully and gain speed as it flies towards the Center.

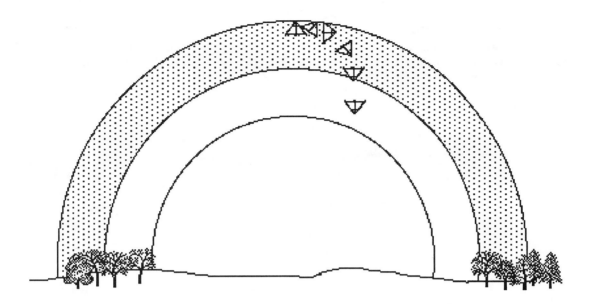

Also, the line pull will increase gradually as the kite's speed increases and it moves back towards the center.

This has illustrated an important fact about control of your stunt kite: THE KITE IS PERFECTLY UNDER CONTROL EVEN IF THERE'S ALMOST NO PULL ON THE LINES ! !

Learn to apply that one fact, and you can make your kite do <u>anything</u>. Applying the right amount of control in the right situation will transform your flying. From just driving around the sky, you can learn to dance.

Now practice hovers <u>everywhere</u> (except over trees):

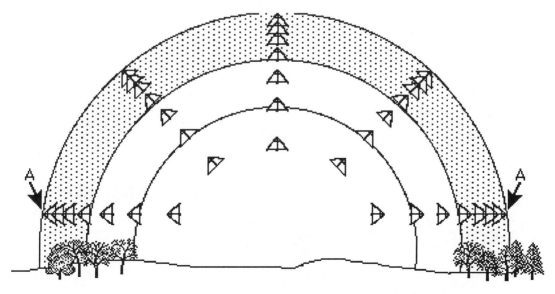

When you do this, you'll discover two things:

1. To do a hover with the kite pointed horizontally (like in the "A" points in the last illustration) you'll need to hold a little "up" line. If the kite is hovering to the right, you'll be holding a little up LEFT; if the kite is hovering to the left, you'll be holding a little up RIGHT. This is because the kite must support its total physical weight. If you are flying a stack that weighs one pound, you'll have to hold one pound of extra pressure "up" on the line.

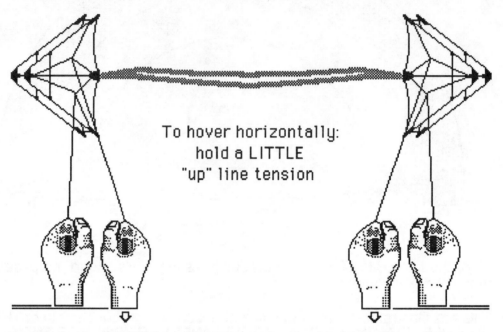

To hover horizontally:
hold a LITTLE
"up" line tension

This actually happens any time you fly horizontally, but there is usually so much line tension that your hands don't notice the small difference. So it feels like "hold even to go straight", even though it's not strictly true.

2. Turning out of a horizontal hover to head back towards the center doesn't work quite the way you might expect. Here's how it works, and why:

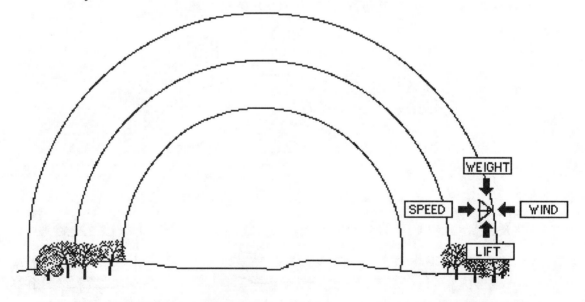

In a hover, everything is in equilibrium. The kite is flying at exactly the same speed as the wind, and is creating just enough lift to support its own weight. Fine, so far.

> *A Foil must be "arched" or "flexed" in order to fly. If the spar is flat rather than flexed, the kite is floating - not flying. In lighter winds, a Foil may have a tendency to float at the hover point. Be careful not to let it float "beyond the edge" and out of the envelope.*

Now, turn out of the hover. Let's turn left, so the kite flies "up and over". Suddenly -- the kite stalls!

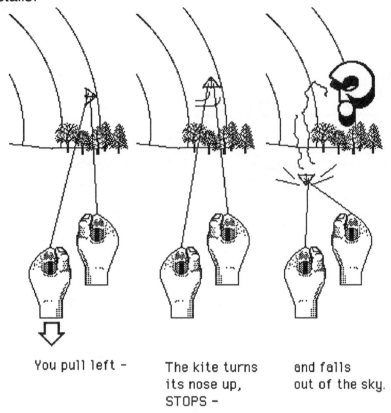

You pull left -   The kite turns   and falls
                       its nose up,   out of the sky.
                       STOPS -

In order to complete a left turn, the kite had to climb. Climbing takes power, just as with an airplane. But remember, in a hover, everything is in equilibrium. The kite is flying at exactly the wind speed, and creating only enough lift to support its own weight. There's no extra power available. And that's why it stalls.

To avoid stalling, you need to ADD SOME POWER to help the kite to climb.

Remember the Better Normal Landing? You walked towards the kite in order to subtract your walking speed from the wind speed and reduce power for a shorter, softer landing. In this situation, do the opposite.

One way you can add power is by taking a couple of steps backwards as you begin your turn. But the more polished technique is to pull back simultaneously with BOTH hands instead of just one.

You may notice that going up and over to the right will "feel" like you're pulling <u>harder</u> with your left hand. What will really happen is that you'll pull with your left hand a fraction <u>before</u> pulling with your right, then bring your right hand even with your left a fraction after your left has completed its pull.

Don't worry, doing it isn't as complicated as explaining it!

Here's how it looks:

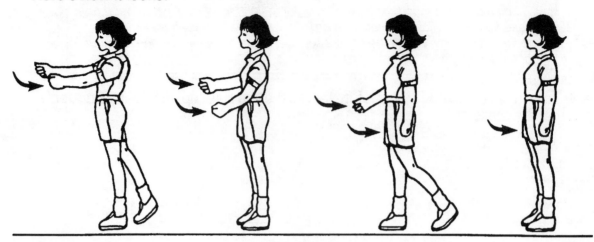

The left hand starts - then the right. Both hands pull. The right finishes even with the left. Notice that the flyer pulls her hands DOWN past her thighs. This allows a longer pull than pulling back to her chest. Also, the weight of her arms helps the pull.

Also notice that a step backward increases speed and control. In fact, moving your feet is almost as important as moving your hands -- and is often more effective.

Here's the other view of the same maneuver:

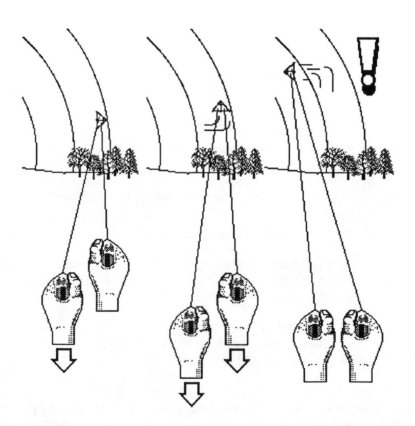

Adding power by pulling or by stepping back is an important concept, and we'll talk about it at length later. For now, use it to help your kite out of hovers, and try it in other situations where your kite needs a little more power.

If you step back, remember to step forward to your original position again later. Pick a time when the kite has plenty of speed and pull, and walk up to where you were. Otherwise, you may find yourself someplace you didn't plan to be!

Now let's turn right from the same hover and go "under". Remember to start with plenty of altitude at first, say 25 feet. Here's what may happen:

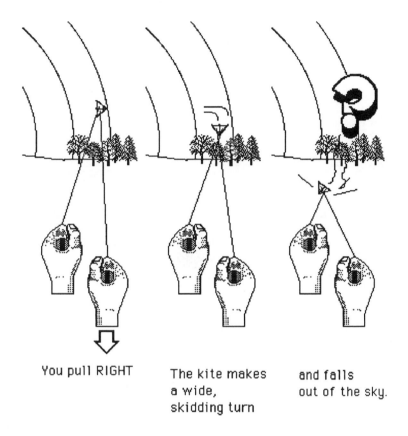

You pull RIGHT

The kite makes
a wide,
skidding turn

and falls
out of the sky.

Now what?! Remember that it's possible to overcontrol. And remember that, the less line is pulling, the less control is required to achieve the same result. When the kite is in equilibrium at a hover, and you PULL RIGHT, you've overcontrolled!

So how do you turn right? PUSH LEFT! That's right, push left. You're holding a little more tension on the left line in order to hold the hover (balancing the weight of the kite, remember?). So relax some of that extra tension, and the result is a nice, neat right turn.

While you are making this turn, there will be almost NO line tension. Finesse is important. Hold your right hand still. This will give the kite a "pivot point" and allow it to maintain stability. Push left just a little, and then HOLD THAT POSITION. It won't "feel" like you're accomplishing anything, but the kite knows what to do.

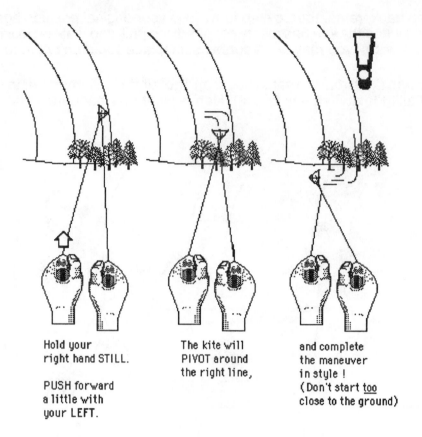

Hold your
right hand STILL.

PUSH forward
a little with
your LEFT.

The kite will
PIVOT around
the right line,

and complete
the maneuver
in style !
(Don't start too
close to the ground)

After you've tried this with plenty of altitude, try starting lower and lower until you're "tucking under" with only inches to spare. It's a sure "gasp getter" if anyone's watching!

AND NOW YOU'RE READY to go exploring. Try anything and everything you can think of, anywhere in the sky that the kite will go. You'll find other situations where you'll want to add power, and also where you'll want to "push" a turn. We'll talk about specific applications of these techniques later. For now, you have all the tools you need to thoroughly investigate the flight envelope, and to make your flying a completely enjoyable experience.

HAVE FUN !

Thrust and lift are the forces that enable a kite to defy gravity. Thrust is created by the velocity of the wind and the kite's speed. Lift is created when bridle and bridle tuning hold the kite at an appropriate angle into the wind.

The correct "angle of attack" causes air to move more slowly across the face of the kite and push upward. At the same time, air moving more quickly across the back of the kite reduces pressure creating a partial vacuum and additional lift.

*Drag pulls back on a kite and gravity pull downward. Gravity is determined by the weight of the kite; drag by its design and the flying angle set by the bridle. Simply put, **a kite must have more lift than drag and gravity to fly**. However, some drag is necessary to give a kite stability. For instance, drag will actually slow a kite down in a dive.*

CHAPTER FIVE: TUNING

The best musician sounds terrible on an instrument that's out of tune. Just as a properly tuned musical instrument gives good sound and great pleasure, a properly tuned stunt kite will delight you with its ability.

The main reasons we tune kites is to adjust for wind conditions, to correct errors, and to maximize performance. In stronger or lighter winds, a kite can be tuned to increase speed, reduce pull, or simply stay in the air. The process is simple if you know what to look for and what to do. So here's --

WHAT TO LOOK FOR:

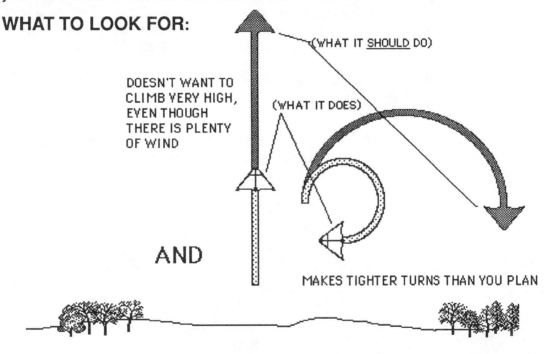

(WHAT IT SHOULD DO)

DOESN'T WANT TO CLIMB VERY HIGH, EVEN THOUGH THERE IS PLENTY OF WIND

(WHAT IT DOES)

AND

MAKES TIGHTER TURNS THAN YOU PLAN

A kite needs tuning when it won't climb well. In any reasonable wind, say 7 MPH, it should climb up to at least a 45 degree angle. The other symptom that goes with "lack of climb" is "turns too tight". The kite will execute very tight turns, and will feel like it's "yanking" itself around, rather that flying smoothly through a turn.

> *You can check your kite's adjustment by holding the bridle clips in your hands with the kite over your head. If the bridle is too low, the kite will not want to lift; too high and the kite will want to float on top of the wind. Find a happy medium.*
>
> ***Robert Loera***
> ***Honolulu, Hawai***

Here's another indication that your stunter needs tuning:

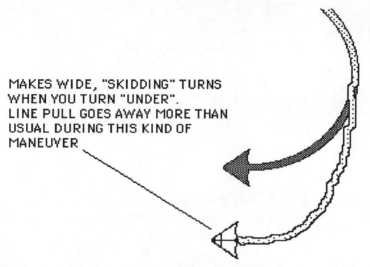

MAKES WIDE, "SKIDDING" TURNS
WHEN YOU TURN "UNDER".
LINE PULL GOES AWAY MORE THAN
USUAL DURING THIS KIND OF
MANEUVER

When the kite makes "down" turns wider than planned, when even the most careful control seems like too much, when the line pull goes away completely and the kite seems on the verge of falling out of the sky -- TUNE IT.

Some kites naturally make noise when they fly. Others are usually silent. The noise (or lack of it) is a valuable indicator of a stunt kite's tuning. Over time, you should learn how to "read" kite noise. We'll talk more about this later.

So now that we've talked about what to look for, let's talk about --

WHAT TO DO

ADJUSTING CLIPS -- Adjusting bridle clips will take a little explaining. You need to know how, why, and when. Let's talk about How first.

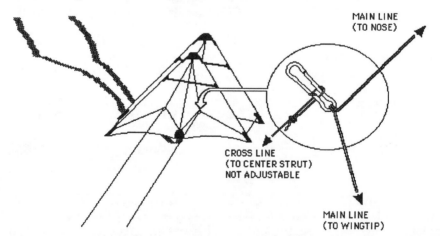

MAIN LINE
(TO NOSE)

CROSS LINE
(TO CENTER STRUT)
NOT ADJUSTABLE

MAIN LINE
(TO WINGTIP)

Stunt kites with bridles use "clips" to attach the flyline. On Diamond Wing stunters, each clip is attached to a single Main Bridle Line. On Delta Wing kites, the clips have two lines attached (besides the flyline) -- the Main Line, which is longer, and the Cross Line. The Cross Line (sometimes called the "Static Line") is not adjustable. With either kind of kite, adjusting the clips consists only of sliding them up or down the <u>Main Line</u>.

"UP" or "FORWARD" or "LIGHTER" means TOWARDS THE NOSE
"DOWN" or "BACK" or "HEAVIER" means TOWARDS THE BASE

Notice that the Main Line has a mark on it. The mark is for reference, to let you know where the clips are on the line. The mark itself is not a "magic" location; it's just there to show you where the clips are <u>in relation</u> to the mark. Read your factory instruction sheet to see what the manufacturer recommends about general clip settings.

This next series of illustrations depicts moving a clip FORWARD.

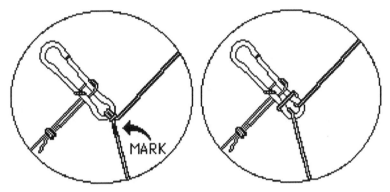

First, loosen the knot by pushing it up the clip as shown.

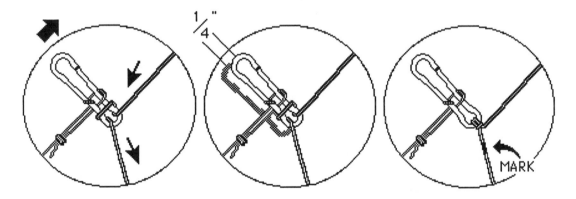

Slide the clip up the line. Make all your adjustments <u>small</u>. Now pull the knot tight again. Notice that the clip is now a quarter of an inch farther forward on the Main Line, as shown by the position of the mark.

A quarter of an inch is plenty, which means that the clips will always be in the immediate vicinity of the mark on the Main Line. The whole range of adjustment, from farthest forward to farthest back, is usually less than ONE INCH, although depending on your kite and the wind conditions, it can change much more. Adjust a little at a time, and fly the kite between adjustments to see what happens.

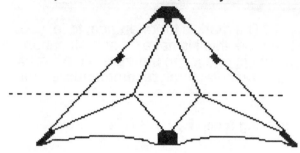

Whenever you adjust, be sure to adjust both clips the same amount. The best way is to position one where you want it, then move the other one to match it. When you're done, both clips must be the same distance from the nose of the kite.

If the clips are different distances from the nose, the kite will require more tension on one line than the other to fly straight. It will also turn tighter in one direction than the other. The kite will act sort of like a car with its front end out of alignment.

The easiest way to check the clips is by eyeball.

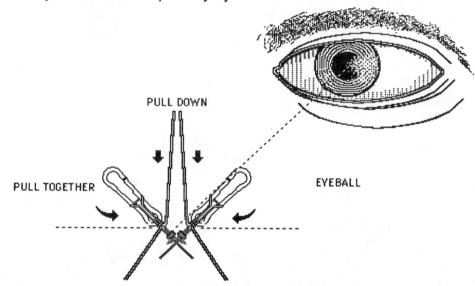

Pull the clips down so that the parts of the Main Line leading from the clips to the nose are taut. Then eyeball the knots to see if they're even. Eyeball accuracy is close enough.

And that's all there is to the <u>How</u> of adjusting clips. Actually doing it should only take about thirty seconds.

> *If your bridle clips seem to be slipping, rub a bit of beeswax on the line and make sure your knot is cinched tight. Don't use candle wax. It doesn't work. Get real beeswax from a hardware store ... or from a bee hive.*
>
> **Sue Taft and Lee Sedgwick**
> **Erie, Pennsylvania**

Now for the reasons Why to adjust: When you adjust the clips, you are changing the kite's <u>angle of attack</u>. The angle of attack is the angle at which the kite meets the wind.

Just as, when sailing a sailboat, you must pull the sail in when it's too loose and let it out when it's too tight, you should adjust your kite to the best angle for the current conditions. Kites are adjusted to a reasonable position at the factory, but you can improve it with a little practice.

Adjustment is also a matter of personal taste. Within a certain range, the kite will fly. How it flies depends on where within that range it is adjusted. Some flyers like tight turns, others like their kite to float around the sky. Most like a mix of both. It's up to you. So please....

DON'T BE AFRAID TO EXPERIMENT ! !

The full range of adjustments will best be found through "trial until error". So adjust the kite a little forward. Then fly it. Then adjust forward some more and fly again. Keep doing that until you're sure you've gone too far. Then do the same with adjusting to the rear. That way you will know what the kite does through its whole range, and will be better able to decide what you like. And if your kite isn't adjusted to suit you, you'll know what to do about it.

> *I tell everyone, "Experiment. You'll learn more and learn it better." Lee (Sedgwick) would have never invented "solo" and "quad" if he hadn't experimented. And don't be discouraged by things that don't work! That's what experimentation is all about.*
>
> *Be especially careful about comments from people who think they know the only "right" way to fly. If no one ever tried anything new, Paul Garber would still be flying box kites.*
>
> **Al Hargus III**
> **Chicago, Illinois**

Finally, let's talk about When to adjust.

In general, WHEN THE WIND GETS STRONGER, you'll need to move the clips BACK. This increases performance, allows sharper turns, and provides more sensitive control, while decreasing the lift of the kite. More wind will be needed to fly out to the sides.

WHEN THE WIND GETS LIGHTER, you'll need to move the clips FORWARD. This provides more lift and improves light wind handling. The kite will make wider turns, climb higher, and fly farther to the sides of the wind, but control will be less sensitive.

We call moving the clips back "setting heavier", because it's for "heavier" wind, and moving the clips forward "setting lighter".

> *If you want to fly in real heavy winds and not put a lot of stress on the kite or yourself, move the clips FORWARD. This allows you to even fly multiple kites in a strong breeze. Your turns won't be as tight, but you also won't have as much pull. Sometimes you don't want to go "skiing" down the field.*
>
> **Sue Taft**
> **Erie, Pennsylvania**

Remember our first tuning example of "What to Look For"? The kite "jerked" itself around turns. The kite didn't climb well and may have been difficult to get off the ground at all. This set of symptoms is an indication that the clips are TOO FAR BACK and need to be MOVED FORWARD.

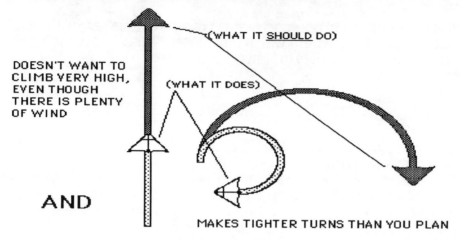

DOESN'T WANT TO CLIMB VERY HIGH, EVEN THOUGH THERE IS PLENTY OF WIND

(WHAT IT SHOULD DO)

(WHAT IT DOES)

AND

MAKES TIGHTER TURNS THAN YOU PLAN

> *Adjusting the length of bridle lines on Delta Wing stunters will also effect their performance. Shorter bridles pull toward the center of the kite; longer bridles pull toward the flyer. If the wings of your kite have a tendency to "flap" or "bounce" in high winds, try lengthening the bridle lines.*

In our second example the kite "skidded" around turns. In an extreme case, it didn't even complete the turn shown here without falling out of the sky. These symptoms indicate that the clips are TOO FAR FORWARD and need to be MOVED BACK.

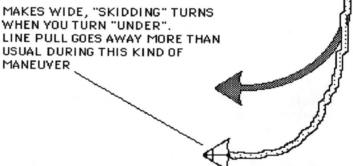

MAKES WIDE, "SKIDDING" TURNS WHEN YOU TURN "UNDER".
LINE PULL GOES AWAY MORE THAN USUAL DURING THIS KIND OF MANEUVER

ABOUT NOISE

Earlier, we promised to talk about noise as an indicator for tuning. Notice that, when the kite flies, it tends to make more noise when it's flying faster. You can use this noise to get an accurate picture of how well the clips are adjusted.

Moving clips forward increases the speed of the kite and the amount of noise. Moving clips back decreases speed and therefore, volume.

Pay attention to the noise your kite makes, and adjust accordingly. You'll find it an easy, accurate method for getting good performance without a lot of hassle.

> *Sometimes, noise can frighten or intimidate people. Never fly too close to roads, sidewalks, on unsuspecting bystanders. It's not that you might hit someone. Just scaring them can hurt the sport.*
>
> ***Corey Jensen***
> ***Monterey, California***

WISKERS or STAND-OUTS

"Wiskers" are thin pieces of solid fiberglass which are installed between the lower cross strut and the base of the sail. They are used primarily to keep the sail tight and prevent collapse or "luffing" at the edge of the wind. Because they hold the kite open, they are also called "stand-outs".

Wiskers improve general performance by increasing the size of the usable wind window and allowing you to fly in lighter winds. They also help with self launches when the kite is laid out flat on it's back and allow some pretty fancy ground maneuvers.

Because stand-outs are not attached permanently to the kite, they're real easy to lose. They are connected to kites in so many ways that its difficult to tell you how to hang onto them the best.

The best advice is to make some extras just in case.

SPECIAL TUNING FOR STACKS

The potential for tuning problems increases dramatically when you start flying multiple kites or "stacks". That makes it a good idea to check your tuning before you launch on any particular day, and to recheck after every landing or crash.

Generally, stacks are flown on a higher bridle settting. Here are few other things to watch for:

First, **Straighten Train Lines**. The lines should run straight between wings without wrapping around wingtips. Wrapped wingtips are very common, and sometimes difficult to spot. In the air, wrapped wingtips will make your kite lean to the side or lean back. Make a habit of including an inspection of your wingtip lines in your Preflight Checklist. Check them every time you launch. If you're flying, and notice your kites leaning, land and check the wingtip lines again.

Second, **Measure Train Lines**. In order to fly together, each wing must be at exactly the same angle to the wind. You know that bridle settings on the lead kite determine its angle of attack. Train lines determine the angles on all the other kites.

Lines stretch. Knots slip. Sometimes, the factory gets sloppy and includes train lines of unequal length. In any case, measuring the lines to make certain they are all equal will improve performance. Also check to be certain that the lines are attached at proper points to each kite.

It's rare for these lines to move during a flying session, so they shouldn't need to be checked before every flight.

Third, **Adjust Bridle Clips**. In general, the more kites your stack has, the less often you'll need to adjust the clips for changes in the wind strength. If the average wind strength shifts significantly during a flying session, you'll see your kite's performance change, and will want to move the clips.

Finally, **Check Vinyl Connections**. This is important. Does your kite have a flexible structure held together by a vinyl nose-cone or connector tubes holding the cross struts? After a crash, the frame parts may have moved in relation to one another. The cross struts may not be in the same place. The nose cones or cross struts may have popped loose.

"Popped" struts at the vinyl connectors are a particular problem in kites where the sails have stretched or lost their sizing. A quick check of the kite will usually turn up any damage.

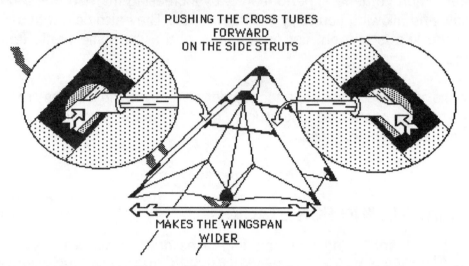

PUSHING THE CROSS TUBES
FORWARD
ON THE SIDE STRUTS

MAKES THE WINGSPAN
WIDER

Wingspans can be adjusted by moving the cross tubes which hold the cross strut. In strong winds, loose tubes will have a tendency to adjust "themselves".

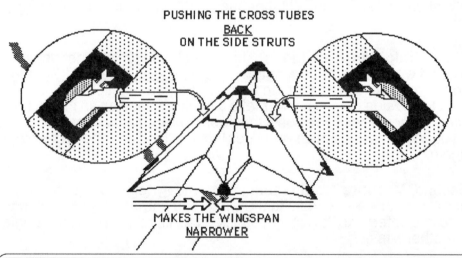

PUSHING THE CROSS TUBES
BACK
ON THE SIDE STRUTS

MAKES THE WINGSPAN
NARROWER

The design of some stunt kites puts more tension or stress on the lower train line than on others. This stress can build up in a stack, stretching train lines and eventually, decreasing the angle of attack on the last kites in the train. The result is "slurring" where the last kites lag behind in a maneuver.

Using train line material with minimum stretch is important. However, if your stack does start to "slur", try shortening the length of the lower train line on the last kite. You can even make field adjustments by using a larkshead knot to insert a short piece of dowel or a stick in the line and "take in" some of its length.

John Waters
Lincoln City, Oregon

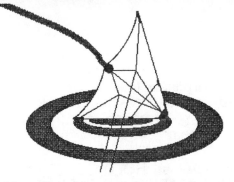

CHAPTER SIX:

ADVANCED FLYING

You've "earned your wings" as a stunt kite pilot. You can launch, fly, and land under reasonably good control. You can tune your kite for varying conditions. And you've definitely progressed past the, " Oh, #$%&*!!!" stage and on to the enjoyment and thrill of the stunting experience.

If you're interested in stunt kites as casual recreation, and it's enough to be able to cruise around the sky and play, you can stop reading now. Our experience, however, is that you'll eventually be bitten by the "high performance bug", and will want to know how to go faster, higher, longer, bigger, stronger, and so on.

So let's move on to the good stuff!

FLIGHT CONTROL

As we just now hinted, there are two ways to fly. There's playing, and then there's practicing. When you're playing, you're just flying. You will tend to stay within your limits as you've already established them, and won't generally try new things. Playing is good for the soul. It takes your mind off whatever might be bothering you, and lets you have some time to....well......play!

Practicing, on the other hand, requires concentration. When you practice, you're concerned with developing your skills. So you'll try new things, and try to do old things better. You'll extend your limits so that the next time you play, you'll be able to play better.

And, of course, there's no reason why playing and practicing can't be mixed into the same flight. Practice awhile, play awhile.

When you did your first Horizontal Eight, that was practicing. Your first Hovers and turns out of Hovers were practice. Here are some more things to practice.

HORIZONTAL PASSES -- Flying almost straight and almost level is easy. Flying "straight and level" is not as easy. It requires concentration and finesse.

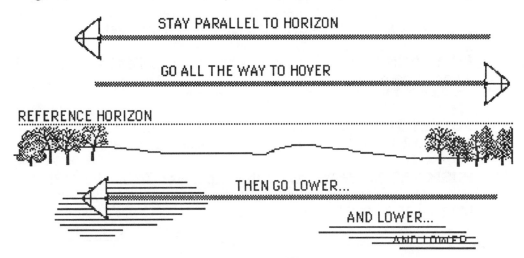

First, establish a "reference horizon" for yourself. This is nothing more than an imaginary line in the sky parallel to the actual horizon. In the figure above, we've used the treetops as markers. Now fly straight as a ruler along, or parallel to, your horizon. You'll probably find that your first attempts have a decidedly "snakelike" look to them.

The secret is: HOLD CONSTANT CONTROL. DON'T STEER ONCE YOU HAVE ESTABLISHED THE LINE. Concentrate on your hands and on what your hands are feeling as the kite flies across. You'll feel the increase and decrease in line tension as the kite flies through variations in the wind. Your hands may move forward and back in response to these. But don't steer. You can even press your forearms together to make sure your hands move forward and back exactly together.

Once you have the idea, try it all the way out to a Hover, then all the way back across to another Hover. Then try it lower. Then try it _lower_. Then try it LOWER. The goal for this practice exercise is to be able to fly all the way across at an altitude of one foot or less.

STRAIGHT FLIGHT -- Now draw _straight_ lines across the sky in _every_ direction. Use just as much concentration and finesse as you did flying six inches from the ground, and make the lines just as straight. As you can already see, the secret to beautiful maneuvers -- to maneuvers that look like you planned them and then did exactly what you planned -- is _concentration_.

THROTTLE CONTROL -- In general, pulling back and pushing forward act like throttle by adding or subtracting power. Controlling throttle is an important part of beauty and grace in flight. And the good news is that you've already had some practice with throttle control, perhaps without realizing it!

Remember that steering and throttle are _two separate things_. STEERING MEANS CHANGING THE RELATIVE TENSION ON THE TWO LINES, WHILE THROTTLE MEANS CHANGING THE TENSION ON BOTH LINES TOGETHER. Often, however, you'll use steering and throttle together. Here are the terms we'll use for the various movements:

> **TURN** - Just like we've been practicing. Pull left to turn left; pull right to turn right.

> **PUSH TURN** - Remember turning "under" from a Hover? You "pushed" left to turn right. That's a Push Turn. A Push Turn slows the kite down through the turn. It also makes the turn tighter than would otherwise be possible, and makes it easier to stop the turn precisely.

> **PULL TURN** - Turning "up" from a hover, you pulled back (and perhaps stepped back) as well as turned. That's a Pull Turn. A Pull Turn accelerates the kite. It also widens the turn.

> **PULL......STOP** - Step back, then stop. Use a Pull Stop to add power and speed just like in a Pull Turn. You pull when doing a Self-Launch.

> **PUSH.....STOP** - Walk forward, then stop. Remember the Better Normal Landing? You walked forward until the kite flew down into the Boundary Layer, then stopped.

Usually when you use throttle, you'll <u>Pull</u> when the kite is climbing and <u>Push</u> when it is descending. You'll see specific examples next.

> *If you have ever wondered how an experienced flyer seems to effortlessly knock out maneuvers with unbelievable ninety-degree turns -- while you're still struggling to not oversteer or draw a good straight line -- it's the push and punch technique that's the secret. If this isn't an integral part of your flying repertoire, it should be. Your flying skills will make quantum leaps forward once you come to grips with the push turn.*
>
> **Abel Ortega**
> **Houston, Texas**

MANEUVER PRACTICE

VERTICAL EIGHTS -- If you fly a Vertical Eight by just doing Turn Left, Turn Right like you did Horizontal Eights, you'll get a "pear shaped" maneuver, bigger on the bottom than on the top. The reason is that the kite flies slower at the top, so the same control produces a sharper turn. A subtle Pull and Push will smooth the maneuver out nicely. Remember the value of finesse.

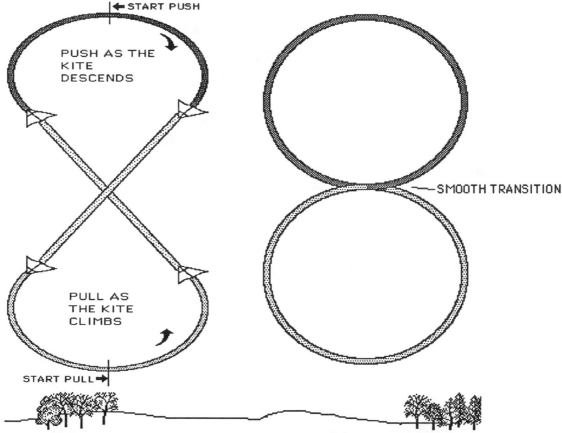

Everything will work about the same for a **ROUND VERTICAL EIGHT** except that you need to watch the transition between Left Turn and Right Turn. Don't "snap" from left to right. Instead, fly the kite smoothly "through" the transition.

Notice that these maneuvers don't have "entry" and "exit" points marked. Make your own, and vary them. Enter from the top or the bottom of the middle. Exit everywhere. Make up your own combinations.

"L's" and SQUARES -- A good "L" is a real crowd pleaser. Begin practice with your horizon well above the ground. Fly straight down, Push Turn, and then fly straight horizontally.

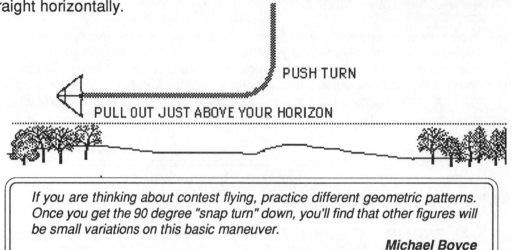

PUSH TURN

PULL OUT JUST ABOVE YOUR HORIZON

If you are thinking about contest flying, practice different geometric patterns. Once you get the 90 degree "snap turn" down, you'll find that other figures will be small variations on this basic maneuver.

Michael Boyce
Berkeley, California

Practice until you can turn just above your horizon. Pushing the dive will slow it down and heighten the suspense, as well as making it easier to turn at the bottom. Practice turning both ways at the bottom. Then put your horizon at ground level and find out if you <u>really</u> got it right!

This Push Turn is your first **"Angle Maneuver"**. If you take the time to get it right, angles, squares, and all their variants will be easy.

One additional hint about making a good 90 degree Push Turn -- just before starting the turn, "lock" your elbow to your side on the "stationary side" of the turn. In the figure above, you'd lock your right elbow since you intend to push with your left hand. Then Push Left and immediately return your left hand even. With a little practice you'll be able to get an exact 90 degree turn every time.

Now use this Push Turn technique four times in a row to do a **SQUARE**.

Once you've mastered 90 degree turns, the only trick to doing a great Square is visualizing a square Square in the sky. Pushing the dive and Pulling the climb helps even it out so it looks more organized, too.

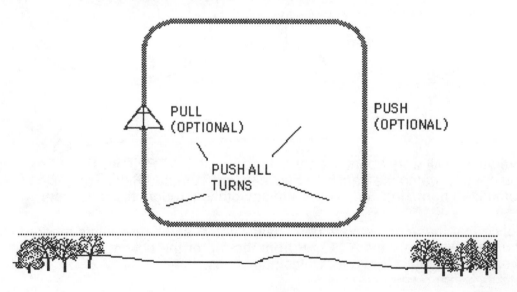

PULL
(OPTIONAL)

PUSH
(OPTIONAL)

PUSH ALL
TURNS

THE "EAGLE" HAS LANDED -- When we first talked about landings, we mentioned the "Eagle". Well, here it is. This maneuver is difficult at first but soon becomes almost second nature. Unfortunately, it only works with the "Delta style" or swept wing stunters.

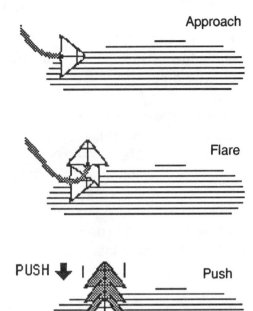

Approach the edge as you would for a normal landing. Remember, walk towards the kite on the approach, then flare to about one foot in altitude. This landing won't work if you flare too high. When the kite has almost stopped, but still has a little forward motion, TURN UP.

What you want the kite to do is pivot its nose vertical and <u>stop in a stall</u> at an altitude of not over 4 feet. Then <u>immediately</u>, PUSH or step forward. The kite will <u>fly backwards</u> down to a landing. Ta-daa!

A perfectly executed "Eagle" landing is a source of wonder for onlookers and also produces great personal satisfaction. If you do it right, keep some tension on the line and you can launch again without further attention. Just remember not to leave the kite staked out unattended.

You can also use this same technique to practice wingtip touches and sustained wing stands.

SPINS -- All stunt kites can turn but not all can spin or turn on one wingtip. It also takes a bit of extra skill to keep the kite under control in a spin.

Spins are really just very tight loops. To complete a spin to the left, PULL LEFT a little more than you would for a loop to the left. HOLD for a few turns, and then bring your hands back even. The kite will fly back out in a straight direction.

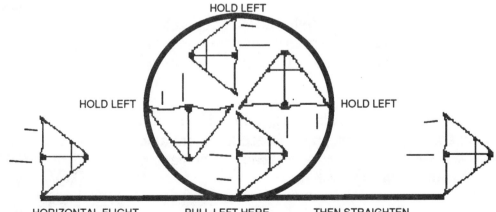

A fast spinning kite will often make a loud roar similar to that of an airplane propeller. (Remember, noise and speed are related.) Many beginners are afraid to put a kite into a spin because it gives the initial impression that the lines will get tangled up. Remember to keep track of the number of turns. Stabilize. And then spin back the other direction.

WING LAUNCH -- Back in Chapter Two, we talked about how to launch a Diamond kite from from a nose-down position. With practice, this same maneuver is possible with Delta Wings as well. The results are spectacular -- not to mention the fact that they save you the trouble of setting up your kite from scratch, every time you crash.

For a wing launch, the kite should be toward the edge of the wind with its nose pointing toward the "outside" of your flying area or away from the center. One wing should be on the ground and the other pointing skyward.

Gently draw back on the upper line so that the wing which is not on the ground beigns to lean toward you. Pull it over just enough for the wind to get under it and and lift the kite. Then pull back sharply on both lines. The nose should swing around into the air, and the kite should lift off after dragging a wingtip for a moment.

If your kite is closer to the center of the wind, you may need to walk left or right to create a better launch angle. A few quick steps backward as you begin to launch will also help. With practice, you will learn to balance your stunter on its nose and lift off without even touching a wingtip to the ground.

> *Just a short note on "Pull" and Push" turning: Try Pushing left while Pulling right. This is usually a very quick move which results in a "flip turn" - 180 degrees or better - almost instantly. It is a "snap-type" maneuver like a "jab". Start with both hands at your body to allow full play in both directions. The kite will usually flip and then return on the same flight line as before the reversal.*
>
> *Cris Batdorff*
> *Manistee, Michigan*

MID-AIR STALLS -- You already know how to hover at the edge of the wind. But what about stopping suddenly in the middle of the wind? With a bit of practice and coordination, a properly tuned Delta can do what we call a "snap" stall.

Start with a horizontal pass. With both hands close to your body, punch one hand forward as if you were going to turn up in a brisk "L". Then, just as quickly, pull your hand back to your body.

Now push <u>both</u> hands forward, hard. These three movements -- punch-pull-push -- need to be done right together. Practice your timing so you can get the maneuver as quick and crisp as possible.

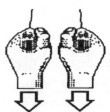

PRACTICE -- Now you have all the tools and techniques for hours of fun and for building contest-quality maneuvers. Try them out. Put them together in your own way. Concentrate. Use finesse. Make the kite do <u>exactly</u> what you have in mind. You'll like the results.

Most of the newer and more fancy tricks work best with a kite that has been tuned "down" or with the clips as far away from the nose as possible. The kite will move slower and stall more easily.

To find your bottom limit, adjust your bridle connection, lowering the clips a quarter inch at a time, until the kite will not launch.

LIGHT WIND FLYING

With the right equipment and techniques, you can keep your kite airborne in as little as 3 mph of wind, and do aerobatics in 5 mph. Here's how:

    1. The lighter the wind, the more important your kite's tuning gets. A poorly tuned kite will fly more or less all right in plenty of wind, but won't fly at all in light wind. So tune your kite. Experiment with clip positions to find the farthest forward adjustment you can get away with.

    2. You'll need LESS STEERING and MORE THROTTLE in lighter wind. Steer carefully, and you'll be able to control the kite even when it's barely moving and has almost no line tension. PULL for climbs and regain position by PUSHING descents.

    3. Switch over to lighter flylines. Remember that heavier line produces drag and reduces control.

ROWING is a technique to keep the kite in the air in the lightest wind. <u>Practice</u> it to get the idea of light wind flying. Then use it on puffy days when the wind sometimes drops off, then picks up again. Rowing to survive a lull in the wind can save you from having to land and wait for more wind.

Here you're using the fact that the kite needs less energy to fly horizontal than it does to climb. Push while flying horizontal then Pull Turn.

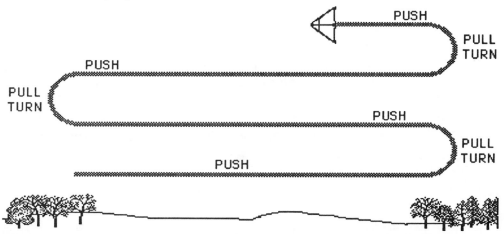

Repeat this process to gain altitude. The result is a climbing "S" turn.

In extremely light wind, you won't be able to gain altitude this way, because the kite won't be able to sustain horizontal flight while you Push. It will lose altitude gradually. The result will be a Horizontal Eight. If you <u>can</u> climb, use the altitude you gain to do maneuvers, then start the climbing turns again. After you've practiced awhile, you'll find you can Row through any maneuver just by Pulling climbs and Pushing descents.

Much of the time you'll be able to row effectively with just your arms, without having to walk forward and back. If you've learned to pull your arms <u>down</u>, rather than back to your chest, it will really pay off now. You'll have better control with less fatigue.

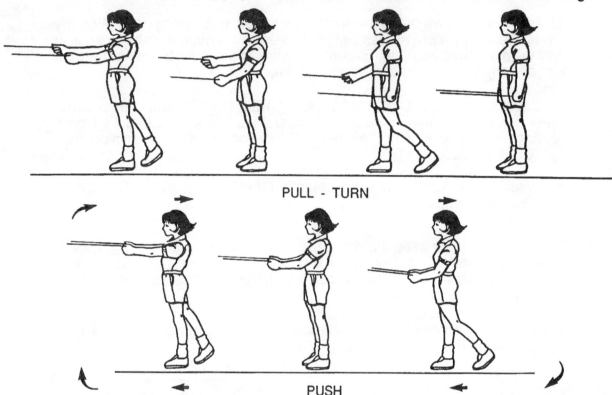

PULL - TURN

PUSH

Rowing is a valuable technique. If you can row, you can fly in just about any wind. You'll also find that the basic technique has other applications that you'll enjoy finding for yourself.

Many manufacturers are now producing "ultra-light" kites or replacement parts. They rely on lighter fiberglass or graphite spars, thinner nylon sails, less reinforcement, and smaller vinyl fittings. Every ounce has been shaved off to allow light wind flight.

Ultralights work well. But because of these adjustments, they tend to be more fragile than standard stunters. If you are hard on kites, stick with a heavier, but more durable version.

HEAVY WIND FLYING

Obviously, as the wind speed goes up, the kite's speed goes up. The kite has more power. The line pull increases, and so does the stress on the kite. In winds over 20 mph or so, some kites are even capable of producing enough stress to break spars and struts, "blow-out" seams, or puncture sails.

Never fly an ultralight kite in heavy winds -- even though it may take the strain. Sails stretch and the kite won't handle right when you try to fly it in lighter winds later.

If you want to go flying in higher winds, here are a few hints on how to minimize the damage.

1. Make sure all your equipment is in good condition. Inspect it carefully. Is the harness frayed where it's attached to the clips? Have the flylines accumulated knots or frays or worn spots? Are there any unpatched tears in the skins? Flying in strong wind will point out weaknesses in your equipment in a dramatic way! Parts are cheap and repairs are easy, so don't neglect them.

2. The first time you launch in strong wind, PULL to get the kite airborne, then PUSH. Walk towards the kite as you fly it up to a hover. As it flies up, look for bending in its frame. From a hover, test the flight envelope a little at a time, putting stress on the kite gradually by venturing closer to the center of the wind. Be prepared to walk towards the kite if necessary to relieve some of the stress.

If the stress seems to be too much for the kite (or for you, for that matter), LAND, and adjust your tuning.

3. De-tune the kite by moving the clips forward. Yes, you're setting it for "less wind", but that's not the point in this situation. Moving the clips forward will prevent the kite from making so much power. It won't turn on a dime, but it will stay together. It will also go terrifically fast, sound like a jet, and be lots of fun to fly.

4. You may want to consider stronger flylines if you intend to spend any length of time flying in winds over 15 mph. See the section about Flylines for more discussion.

High wind flying puts tremendous stress on the center spine of most stunt kites. Try replacing the center rod with stronger fiberglasss or graphite. You can also use an insert of fiberglass or wood.

The extra weight won't make much difference in heavy winds and the added support will keep the kite from "warping" while flying or breaking on impact with the ground.

Hoy Quan
Montebello, California

BODY POSITION - And a word about <u>your</u> frame and <u>your</u> limits. Almost any stunt kite in 25 mph winds <u>will drag you around</u>. Work up to flying monsters in strong wind gradually, or you'll get the same results as if you overdo any other vigorous exercise. You'll bend <u>your</u> frame!

When you're flying a powerful kite in lots of wind, brace yourself properly.

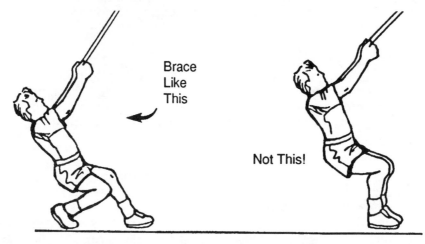

Brace Like This

Not This!

If something breaks, or the wind suddenly drops, the flyer on the right is going to be dealt a severe blow to his . . . pride. And a broken . . .pride . . . is very painful and takes a long time to heal!

Keep your weight low and one foot back, ready to catch yourself if necessary. If you use the correct position, the kite can actually drag you forward without pulling you over on your face. You can lean against the line when the kite is pulling hard, then regain your balance when it slacks off.

For more about heavy wind flying, see the sections on Tuning and Flylines. There you'll find information about equipment and adjustments that will make it easier on you and your kite when the wind gets excited.

CHAPTER SEVEN:

ALL ABOUT FLYLINES and RODS

SELECTING THE "RIGHT LINE"

Many stunt kites come with line included. Others require you to purchase line separately.

Sooner or later, you'll probably end up buying additional line, either because the original line broke, because you're looking for more performance, or because you want more variety for different flying conditions.

Here are five things to think about when picking flylines:

1. **STRENGTH** - Obviously line that's too weak won't work. The bigger the kite or the stronger the wind, the stronger your lines will have to be.

2. **STRETCH** - The less your lines stretch when you pull, the more precise your control will be.

3. **DIAMETER** - Diameter makes drag, and drag makes sag. Sag degrades control. And here's a sad fact of life, aerodynamically speaking:

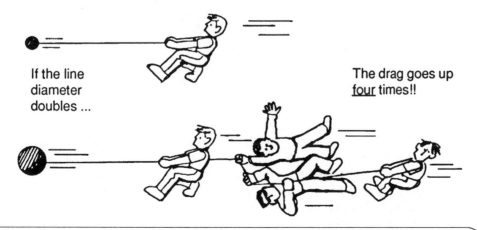

If the line diameter doubles ...

The drag goes up <u>four</u> times!!

No <u>one</u> line is best for all conditions. It is best to use the smallest diameter, but strongest line you can for any particular wind. But consider the value of your kite along with the wind strength. Don't risk a valuable kite on the wrong flying line.

Since objects with round cross sections produce more drag for their thickness than streamlined ones, the lines actually can produce more drag than the kite itself! Increased line drag shows up generally in lower performance such as slower kite speeds or higher wind requirements. Its most apparent effect is sag.

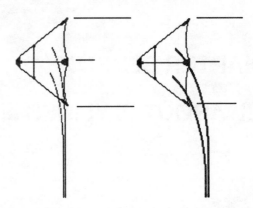

Excess sag creates slack that needs to be taken up as you pull the controls before the kite responds. It's like driving a car with loose steering. And the sag tends to pull the kite's nose in, making control of its angle of attack less precise.

4. **DURABILITY** - Some types of line last longer. Others will fray or wear faster depending on the conditions they're used in. We'll discuss durability when we talk about specific line types.

5. **COST** - Don't be surprised by the expense of good quality flying line. You will find tremendous variation among the types available.

The one item in this list about which there's no compromise is strength. If you mess around with line strength, you'll end up with broken lines. UNDERSTRENGTH LINES ARE <u>DANGEROUS</u>.

> *Remember to burn or melt the ends of your line. Not only does this prevent fraying, it also creates a "stopper" which keeps the end of the line from slipping through a knot.*
>
> *Lee Sedgwick*
> *Erie, Pennsylvania*

The ideal flying line would have zero stretch for responsiveness, be as thin as possible to minimize wind resistance, be lightweight, be strong and durable to resist breakage, and cost next to nothing. Well, they say life is full of compromises. So is kite flying. Here is a rundown on the major types of stunt flying line.

Remember that braided lines are thinner and stronger than twisted ones, but also a bit more expensive.

SPECTRA - Smooth, lightweight, thin, and slippery, Spectra has become the preferred line for most stunt flying. It is excellent for team flying or performing numerous spins. It's also so light that it floats and is available in several colors besides the standard white. Spectra's main weakness is a low melting point which means that contact with other types of line will burn or cut through it. That means you must be careful if other flyers are using something else. Spectra may also require special sleeving for knots.

KEVLAR - This is a synthetic material characterized by its ultra-fine, yellow fibers. Kevlar is very thin for it's strength, stretches less than Dacron (3% versus 10% at 2/3 rated load), and is reasonably durable. It's main drawbacks are higher cost, abrasiveness - it can cut other lines and people - and the fact that knots in Kevlar require special attention. (More on knots later.) Kevlar also breaks down after prolonged exposure to sunlight.

NYLON and DACRON - Nylon is one of the least expensive but worst materials to use because of its stretch. Nylon expands like a rubber band. Although many inexpensive kites come supplied with nylon, do yourself a favor and replace it. Dacron is reasonably priced, durable, and tolerable in the stretch department but is seldom used because of thiner, less elastic alternatives.

New flylines usually have to be set up. This includes tying loops at the ends, stretching, and making both equal lengths. Start by tying the loops in one end of each line. Then attach those loops to the same point on a stationary object.

Stretch the lines out before finishing the other ends. Pull as hard as you think your kite will without exceeding the line breaking strength, and apply this pressure for several minutes. If the line breaks at this point, you probably have defective line.

Once the lines are strectched, pull them tight again and adjust one or the other until they occupy the same lateral position. Then give a little slack and see whether both lines droop to the same position. Once the lines are stretched equally, just mark the ends, trim any extra, and finish them off with loops .

Robbi Sugarman
Mill Neck, New York

HOW MUCH LINE?

Stunt kites will fly on anywhere between 50 and 400 feet of line. Most commercially packaged flying line comes in 150 foot lengths. The amount you should actually use depends on several factors.

THE LONGER THE LINE IS, THE MORE IT WILL STRETCH. More stretch means less control or responsiveness. A 150 foot line will have 50 per cent more stretch than a 100 foot line.

Short lines take less time to wind up; longer lines require a larger flying field.

The important thing to remember is that kites flown on shorter lines will <u>appear</u> to be faster and more responsive. They don't actually move faster, but because the kite requires shorter distances to complete a maneuver, that maneuver will seem to occur more quickly and take faster reactions to control.

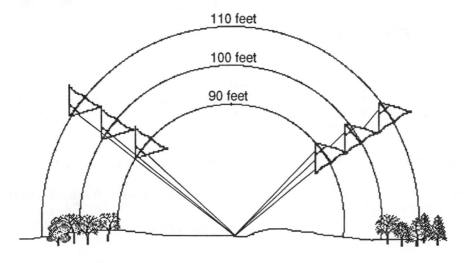

110 feet

100 feet

90 feet

WHAT WEIGHT?

Many manufacturers recommend a specific weight of line for their kites. However, the best weight of line for a given situation will depend not only on the kite used, but also on the wind, the number of knots, and the length used.

Line weight and length is usually printed on the packaging. Don't forget to write these figures down before you throw the packaging away.

Many experienced flyers will carry a variety of lines for use with different kites and wind conditions. They will attempt to use the lightest and thinnest possible line in different circumstances for maximum performance.

KNOTS and SLEEVING

Any knot is a <u>weak spot</u> in the line. Most knots will reduce the strength of flying line by up to 40 percent. If you use knots, we recommend a simple OVERHAND KNOT for end loops. This knot has about 80 percent of the strength of the line. In other words, on a 90 pound line, the knot will hold roughly 72 pounds.

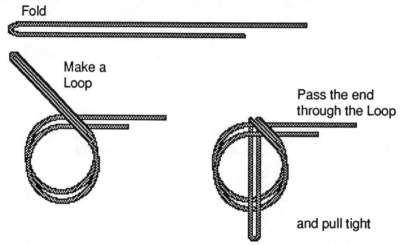

Fold

Make a Loop

Pass the end through the Loop

and pull tight

You can use a knot with more strength, but you risk overstressing the line. Then, it could break anywhere. This way, if you break a line, it will break at the knot. You'll be able to tie a new loop and go on flying, rather than losing an entire set of lines.

Some types of "high tech" lines can't handle knots at all. Spectra, because of its low melting point, and Kevlar, because of its abrasiveness, will actually wear through at points where knots are tied. You'll need to sleeve the line to prevent breakage.

Sleeving or "padding" involves inserting the line through a seven or eight inch long protective cover or sleeve.

The easiest way to sleeve lines is by using a thin piece of solid wire folded in half. Slip the folded end of the wire through the sleeve, insert the line through the top loop (like threading a needle), and pull your line through the sleeve. Then tie a knot in the protected portion of the line.

Remember to melt the ends of the sleeve and line to prevent fraying.

Sleeving material and wire is often included with commercially produced line. Generally speaking, if you aren't using special products like Spectra or Kevlar, sleeving isn't necessary unless you plan to exceed 60 per cent of the line's rated strength.

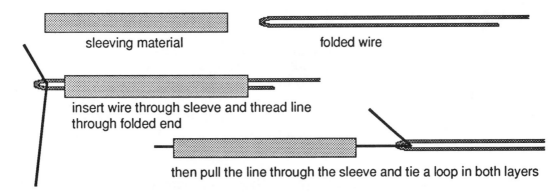

sleeving material

folded wire

insert wire through sleeve and thread line
through folded end

then pull the line through the sleeve and tie a loop in both layers

RODS FOR YOUR FRAME

Under normal wind conditions, your flying performance is based 75% on skill and 25% on your equipment. In heavier winds, and particularly in light winds, that ratio changes to 50% for equipment. Lighter winds need lighter equipment; heavier winds need stronger kites. This means that the frame of your kite, which provides much of its strength and most of its weight, is very important.

The rods used in kite frames can be very confusing. There are different types of materials, different sizes, different manufacturers and lots of funny names and codes. But if you lose or break your original rods, you need to replace them with the same type in order to maintain the balance and flexibility of the kite.

Kite rods can be evaluated according to their stiffness, strength, weight, and cost. As with flying line, there are compromises. Stronger rods are better in a crash, but heavier. Stiff and lightweight rods fly better but are more expensive.

The materials currently available and used in kites are made from fiberglass, graphite, and aluminum/carbon composits. Here's a brief explanation of each:

FIBERGLASS - has the advantage of being strong and relatively low in cost but is also heavier. Usually, fiberglass rods are manufactured as arrow shafts and marked according to the weight of the bow that the arrows match. A very popular rod is the "K75" which was originally made for a 75 pound bow.

PULTRUDED GRAPHITE - is stiffer for its weight, or lighter for a given stiffness, than fiberglass. It is also more expensive and not as strong. "Pultruded" is a manufacturing term which is a combination of extruding and pulling. Each manufacturer has a different way of grading their products, often based on their outside diameter.

SPIRAL WOUND GRAPHITE - With pultruded rods, the fibers line up along the length of the shaft. Spiral wound rods have some fibers wrapped around the rod in a spiral fashion. This process makes them much stronger and stiffer, but also much more expensive. Spiral wound rods are usually graded by a pair of numbers indicating the diameter and the number of layers of graphite. For the same number of layers, a larger diameter is stiffer.

ALUMINUM/CARBON COMPOSITS -- Here, graphite fibers are bonded to an aluminum tube to provide more support. These rods are comparable to graphite in stiffness. They are a bit stronger than pultruded graphite, but not as strong as spiral wound. Rods are sized according to the number of layers of graphite, and the diameter of the aluminum. A "3-30" has three layers of graphite on a .230 inch aluminum tube. The rods that are made specifically for kites are called "A/C/K" for Aluminum/Carbon/Kite.

FLYLINE TROUBLESHOOTING

There are some things you can do to avoid flyline trouble. With proper care and attention, a set of flylines will give long and faithful service.

WATCH FOR FRAYING. The more often you drag your lines across rocks or sharp objects, the more often you cross lines with another flyer, the more trees you eat, the quicker your lines will fray. You can prolong the life of your flylines considerably just by being careful.

Be particularly concerned about fraying about two inches from the end knots. This is one place that wear and tear tends to build up. Inspect your lines occasionally, and if you see significant fraying at this spot, cut the ends off and tie new loops. You'll break fewer lines in the air that way.

AVOID TANGLES. The most common problem, and by far the most aggravating, is getting the flylines all tangled up. A badly tangled set of lines can take hours to undo, and can spoil your whole day. It's far better to know some techniques for handling line to stay clear of tangles in the first place.

The next few pages will describe a few procedures for avoiding tangles in some common flying situations.

Keep "twist" out of the lines. The twist we're talking about here isn't the two lines getting twisted over one another while you fly. It's twist in the individual lines. Look closely at your flylines. If they are of braided construction, they won't be perfectly round. You'll be able to see whether there's twist in the line, or whether it's straight.

Twist is bad for two reasons. First, it coils the line like a spring. That lets it stretch more, making control response worse when you fly. Excess twist will actually shorten your lines or alter the length of matched lines.

Secondly, it encourages tangles whenever the lines are slack. If your lines are badly twisted, they'll try to tangle at every opportunity. Ground handling will be more difficult. So will winding up your lines. And if you get the lines tangled up, they'll be <u>much</u> harder to undo.

The simplest, best way to keep twist out of your lines is to use a good snap swivel at one end and follow a standard procedure for winding them up. Wind up in the same way you unwound when you laid your equipment out. Stand in one place while winding, and let the line drag towards you. That way, the line will untwist as you reel in. (See Packing Up in Chapter Three for more details.)

Develop good habits for winding up your line. If they are twisted now, fix them. Then if the twists come back, you'll know you're still winding up wrong.

Spectra line is slippery and can slide or "creep" even through a knot in the sleeving. Creeping will effect the length of matched lines and also reduce the size of your end loop. What's the answer? Simple. Tie <u>two</u> knots in your sleeving.

Be Smart Around Obstacles. We've seen flyers do some amazing things to try to get their lines out of a tree. As with many other problems, the right way is simple, once you think about it.

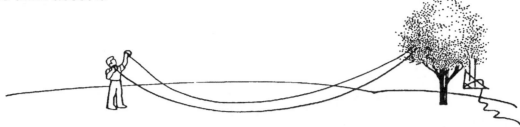

Disconnect the kite and clips from the lines. Pull the lines straight out of the tree. Then reconnect, and fly some more. If the kite lands in the top of the tree, try pulling it out with the lines. The kite will withstand a fairly hard pull before anything breaks. Even if something does break, it's often better to have to replace a strut or two rather than climb the tree.

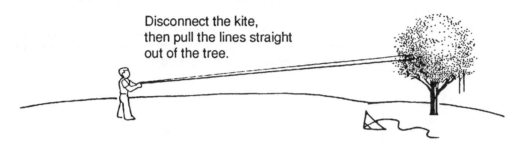

Disconnect the kite, then pull the lines straight out of the tree.

> *Set up your kite twenty feet from the closest obstacle. Unwind your lines - attach your handles - set down the rest of your gear - and fly. Whenever you approach your gear, you'll know that you're twenty feet from the obstacle.*
>
> **Corey Jensen**
> **Monterey, California**

Learn How to Fly with Others. The most common problem is getting your lines crossed with someone else. There are two "right ways" and one "wrong way" to share a flying field.

RIGHT WAY #1. The simplest way to enjoy yourself safely is to stay away from other flyers. Make sure you're far enough apart that your lines can't cross. This way, you'll have enough space to fly without worrying.

Of course, it takes a lot of space to fit very many flyers onto a field this way, and many fields are just too small. If you are flying with friends, you don't get to see much of each other. And besides, you're likely to end up a long way from the picnic lunch.

These drawbacks will tempt you to fly closer to others, but be careful you don't end up doing it the wrong way.

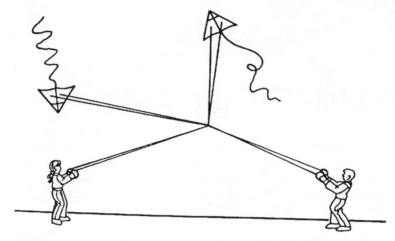

WRONG WAY: Two flyers who cross lines while standing some distance apart are almost always guaranteed to tangle and crash. The two sets of lines "wind each other up", and both kites go out of control.

RIGHT WAY #2: If you like to fly together, stand nearly shoulder-to-shoulder. You'll find that, if you cross lines, your flylines will twist over each other just like they do when you do a loop. You'll both still have control, and will be able to fly out of the twist. Just be sure to remember how you got into the twist, so you can reverse it to get out!

Flying together like this requires concentration, because you'll need to pay attention to where the other kite is as well as your own. It also creates all the exciting possibilities for formation aerobatics. We'll talk about how to get started flying formations later. For now, just give it a try. If possible, fly with others regularly. Better still, find a regular partner to practice with. Talk about what you're doing. You'll soon discover that flying together opens the door to wonderful new levels of aerial excitement.

HANDS AND HANDLES

Handles are an important part of your flying equipment. The right handles can make your flying easier and more precise. The wrong handles can be dangerous.

The perfect flying handles are:
Strong, Safe, Comfortable, and, preferably -- Inexpensive!

They should also be light weight. Line under pressure stretches. If you let go of the handles while the lines are under heavy load, the lines will "slingshot" the handles forward for a considerable distance. Under those circumstances, lightweight handles are much less likely to cause injury to someone who happens to be in their path. Also, light handles won't travel as far.

There are four predominant types of handles being used currently for stunting:

Padded Handles - generally recognized as offering the best feel and control for precision flying. Don't confuse them with the cheap wooden handles which are occasionally packaged with kites. Get rid of those uncomfortable wooden "sticks". Buy yourself a pair of good, sturdy, lightweight padded handles.

Halo Spools - look like small plastic tire rims. Halos are useful because you can easily adjust the amount of line you use or even let out more line after a launch. Halos are also convenient line winders. In heavier winds, you have to grip them hard unless all the line is all out or they will slide in your hands.

Molded Plastic Handles - available in a variety of styles. Some allow you to trim extra line by wrapping the excess around the handle. Plastic handles tend to be hard on the hands with a strong pulling kite because there is no padding. You'll also sacrifice a little sensitivity of control because you won't be able to "feel" the line quite as well, but for most flying that won't be a problem.

Straps and Harnesses - work well with strong pulling kites but sacrifice some feel or control. The strap transfers the pull that normally would be supported by the fingers to the wrist, lessening fatigue and allowing longer flights with bigger kites. A harness transfers the load to your waist. For really big kites or stacks, consider padded straps. And with any harness, look for a safety release that lets you get loose FAST.

Think about the size of your hands when you go shopping for handles. My hands are small so larger spools and handles are harder to hang onto. You might consider wearing gloves. One nice thing about Halos is that they come in different sizes.

Halos are also useful because you don't have to use all your line. You can launch on short lines and even adjust your line length while the kite is in the air. Just slacken your grip on the spool and let the line "spin" out. Remember to make sure you let both lines out evenly so they remain the same length. And be careful you don't let them spin so fast you burn your hands or let out so much line that you might hit obstacles or other flyers.

Susan Gomberg
Lincoln City, Oregon

Wrist straps first appeared in about 1983, and were hailed as a major advance in kite flying. Then flyers who regularly used wrist straps began complaining of numb fingers and pain in their hands.....when they weren't flying. Several eventually sought medical attention, and found that they had acquired Carpal Tunnel Syndrome.

What's **CARPAL TUNNEL SYNDROME**??

Funny you should ask... The human wrist is a marvel of engineering. Its structure of 9 or 10 small bones with tongue-twisting names allows the wrist its amazing flexibility and its ability to support heavy loads -- like when you fly with handles.

The wrist does its job very well. But it was not designed to be squashed together, and that's exactly what a wrist strap does. Pushed out of alignment, the Carpal Bones of the wrist compress the Carpal "Tunnel" and mash the Median Nerve. Sounds messy and is. Even a mild case is very uncomfortable.

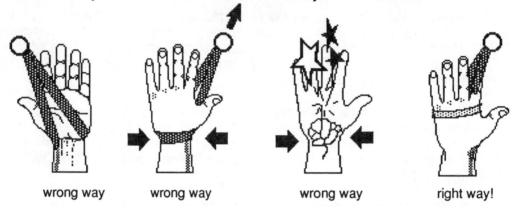

| wrong way | wrong way | wrong way | right way! |

The answer to flying properly with straps is to take pressure off the wrist by wrapping it around the <u>back of your hand</u> and <u>extending the strap between two fingers</u> rather than between the finger and thumb. It's that simple.

> *Padded* straps work better. They don't cut into your hand or cut off circulation. Be sure your straps are loose enough that you can shake them off or slip your hands out quickly in an emergency.
>
> **Sue Taft**
> **Erie, Pennsylvania**

No matter what you use for handles, after you've been flying for a while on any particular day, especially if you're flying a strong pulling kite or train, your fingers will get tired. Land and rest your hands. How long it takes to wear your fingers out depends on several things: your grip strength and the condition of your hands, the comfort of the handles, size of the kite, and wind strength. You can influence a couple of these factors if you want to be able to fly longer at a time.

Several flyers we know exercise their hands regularly with one of those exercisers that looks like a spring with two handles attached. They claim it helps, and they're probably right. Of course, regular flying will achieve the same result.

Finally, and perhaps most important is this central rule about kites and handles:

If you can't hang on to it, you shouldn't be flying it !!

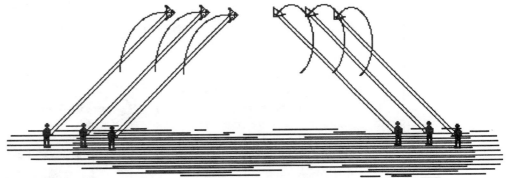

CHAPTER EIGHT:
HIGH PERFORMANCE FLYING

High performance flying involves all of the different innovations and variations that stunt kites allow. Before the ink is dry on this page, someone will have concocted something new. But that being said, let's talk about some of the things that are being done today.

LARGE STACKS

Almost any stunt kite can be stacked by attaching multiple kites together at the bridle point. Stacking kites will increase pull by increasing total surface area. It will also slow the kite down a bit because of the additional drag.

> *No matter how large your set gets, it will only require additional support on the base kite. Stunt kites are designed so that stresses are distributed linearly through the stack. In English, that means that each kite except the Base Kite only has to worry about flying itself, and doesn't get stresses from any of the other kites.*
>
> **Rick Bell**
> **San Diego, California**

If you plan to experiment with stacked kites, here are a few things to keep in mind:

1. The most common problem with kite trains is lines wrapped around wings. Before each launch, check the train lines between each kite. If you are flying and notice the stack leaning, land and check the lines again.

2. Try experimenting with different length train lines. Depending on the kite you are flying, shorter lines may increase your control or decrease tangles. Shorter spacing on long trains also reduces pull.

3. Reinforce the lead kite and train lines on longer stacks.

4. Check your tuning regularly. Train lines should be of equal length and should be inspected periodically for stretch.

> *As a general rule, the best length for train lines on a large stack is the length of the kite's leading edge.*
>
> **Lee Sedgwick**
> **Erie, Pennsylvania**
>
> *Sedge lies! None of his train lines are that long!*
>
> **Al Hargus III**
> **Chicago, Ilinois**

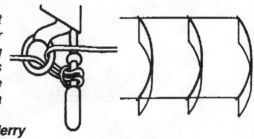

There are many methods for attaching kites together in stacks. For larger or heavier pulling kites, a line-to-line connection is stronger and also provides for easy disconnection and kite replacement.

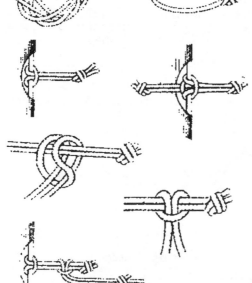

Use small loops or "nooses" at each bridle point. The loops are created using a simple overhand knot.

The loops are wrapped around the kite's frame with a larkshead. Push the knotted end through the loop and pull it snug. One loop is needed on the back kite. The front and intermediate kites take two. You may need to tape the loops in place to avoid slippage.

A second larkshead can be used to attach the ends of the train or bridle lines to the loops. Slip the larkshead over the overhand knot and pull it snug. Then slide the larkshead up to the overhand "stopper" knot.

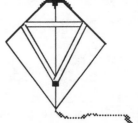

POWERFLYING

When you can feel the pressure of the wind on your kite, you are involved in what we call Powerflying. This means, of course, that virtually everytime you step onto the flying field, you're doing powerflying to some degree. What we're talking about here, however, is adding additional sail, or flying in much higher wind than normal to PURPOSELY LIFT OR PULL YOURSELF with your kites.

Powerflying can be DANGEROUS. People who do it are usually experienced flyers who know exactly what to expect from their equipment and themselves. If you are new to Powerflying, DON'T DO IT ALONE. Take a helper.

> *Some people power fly with 300 pound flylines but only 200 pound bridles. You have to always be careful about bridles. They really take a beating and need to be checked regularly.*
>
> **Lee Sedgwick**
> **Erie, Pennsylvania**

Kites used for powerflying usually fall into two categories; smaller, faster kites which are usually flown in long stacks, and larger, slower kites flown singly or in groups of up to six. A faster kite will reach and pass through the "power zone" at the center of the wind much more quickly that a larger slower one. The smaller kite will also give a very strong pull that will tend to diminish quickly. For a sustained pull, a slower kite is better because it stays in the power zone longer. You can also use longer lines to get up into fresher and more constant breezes.

When kites are flown in large stacks, or when the wind comes up, skilled flyers can do some amazing things. Sleds, wagons, or small boats can be pulled; flyers can "ski" across the ground; leaps of better than ten feet into the air can be attained! But remember, **POWERFLYING CAN BE DANGEROUS**.

1. Kites and train lines must be in good repair. Train lines in particular need to be reinforced to stand the strain of your additional weight.

2. Any harness or handles used must have a quick release system in case of an emergency.

3. Make sure that no one is downfield. The concern about hitting someone with a large or fast kite is obvious. Remember also, that if you need to use your harness release, a "flying" harness, handles, or control bar can be more dangerous than the kite. If you have to let go, be careful!

4. Lines are particularly important. In no case should you attempt to powerfly on lines with less than 300 pounds of strength. Lines and connections should also be checked regularly for stress and weakening.

ALWAYS DOUBLE CHECK YOUR EQUIPMENT. If you use common sense and good safety procedures, you can powerfly at a significantly reduced risk.

> *Some current "powerflying" records:*
> *Largest Stunt Kite: 718 square feet*
> *Longest Stunt Kite Train: 253 kites*
> *Fastest Kite: 120 m.p.h. (verified by police radar gun).*
> *Most Consecutive Spins in one direction: 250*

FORMATION or "TEAM" FLYING

One of the best ways to share your flying space is to fly together in a team or formation. Although team flying is more difficult than flying alone, it's great fun and the results are spectacular. Besides, it's not as hard as most people think if you take the right approach.

Taking the right approach means two things -- organizing your equipment and then organizing the team.

> *Want to put together a great flying team? Be prepared to practice for hundreds of hours - and possibly lose friends or even get a divorce because of it. Team flying can be fun, but it takes commitment and all of your free time if you want to be good.*
>
> ***Al Hargus III***
> ***Chicago, Illinois***

LINE ADJUSTMENTS for TEAM FLYING -- Back when we talked about wind, we mentioned that kites, like other obstacles, create turbulence. When you're flying in formation, you quickly notice that turbulence from other kites makes smooth performance very difficult. To solve that problem, EACH FLYER SHOULD FLY ON DIFFERENT LENGTH LINES.

First decide who is going to be the leader. This person's lines are the longest. Then each successive flyer's lines should be three to five feet shorter than the person who will be flying in front of them.

One hundred and fifty feet is usually a good length to start with. The line lengths will then be 150', 145', and 140' for a three person team. Not only does this eliminate turbulence, it also keeps the kites from colliding in the air if someone makes a mistake.

Of course, that will <u>never</u> happen to you...

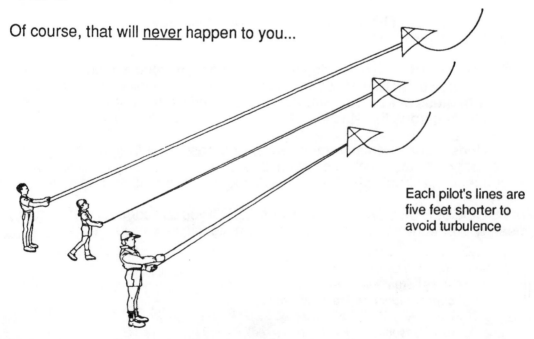

Each pilot's lines are five feet shorter to avoid turbulence

Now that your lines are all set, you need to tune your kites.

TUNING -- Because your lines are set at different lengths, each kite will appear to travel at a different speed. Actually, as we said earlier, the kites aren't moving at different speeds, but are traveling different distances. The result from the flyer's point of view is that they look like they are flying different speeds.

On a three person team, the lead kite will have to travel four percent further than the last kite to get from one side of the field to the other. By changing bridle settings, you can adjust the speed of each kite so they stay together in maneuvers.

Bridle settings were discussed in detail in the Chapter on Tuning. Generally, you move the bridle clips toward the nose for more speed and away from the nose for less speed. Trial and testing are the only ways to get all team kites moving together.

> *When you first set-up to team fly, set all bridles the same. In medium to high winds, subtle speed differences between the kites may be noticed. The last kite (on shortest lines) will probably be fastest. Take time to experiment with bridle settings to get all kites flying together. It will be worth it in the long run.*
>
> **Rod Guyette**
> **Tacoma, Washington**

TEAM ASSIGNMENTS -- Each team member has different responsibilities in organized team flight. The first or "lead" flyer announces maneuvers and calls out each turn. The leader is responsible for safety and must also make sure each team member is lined up and in position before a maneuver is called.

The middle or "intermediate" flyers are the pace setters. Locked in between the front and back, the intermediate flyers must try to balance speed and spacing. They use arms and body movements for throttle control.

The last or "tail" flyer is also responsible for adjustments. Besides flying the called maneuvers, they must match the spacing between the other kites.

TEAM MANEUVERS -- There are three basic kinds of maneuvers that can be flown by teams ...

> **Follow the Leader** -- Each flyer follows directly behind the one in front of them through each of the maneuvers.

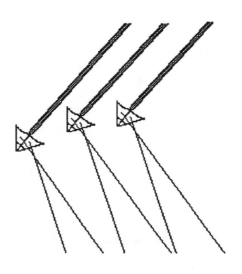

Synchronized Flying -- All flyers turn at the same time when the command is given by the leader.

Opposing Maneuvers -- Team members separate, and then fly toward each other. They either recover at the last moment or "thread the needle" to avoid a collision.

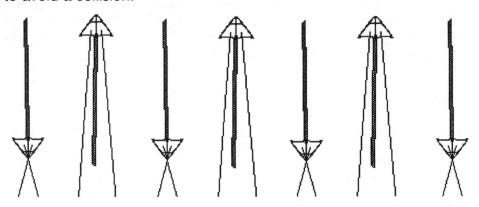

The Top of the Line Team prepares maneuvers using "practice sticks". These dowels have a small paper "kite" at one end and a loop of string at the other.

When "practicing", the team stands in normal flying position and moves each kite as it would normally be flown. This helps identify each flyer's position and timing. We place our wrists through the loop of string, and "turn" the kites by rotating the dowels in our fingers. When each kite finishes a maneuver, the pilot can look at the loop and see if they would normally have any twists left in their flyline.

Practice sticks save a tremendous amount of time since they allow teams to "talk through" and prepare new maneuvers while still on the ground.

Ron Reich
San Diego, California

In the next Chapter, we'll discuss some of the maneuvers that are flown at stunt kite competitions. In the meanwhile, relax and use your imagination...

The type of flyline you use makes a big difference in high performance flying. A tight, smooth weave is better for team flying so that the lines can slide when they twist around each other. In Power Flying, a looser weave is better. But use a loose weave line in Solo Flying, and you can really feel the abrasiveness as it slides through the dog stake.

Lee Sedgwick
Erie, Pennsylvania

"SOLO" FLYING

"Solo" or "Dog Stake" Flying is a term used to describe flying while DOWNWIND of your kite. Some people call it Reverse Flying. To do this, you thread your flylines through some stationary upwind "hook". Often, solo flyers use one of those corkscrew-type dog leash holders. That's how we got the term "Dog Stake" Flying.

> *The best thing we can say about solo flying is that you have to go out by yourself -- you have to concentrate on what you're doing -- and eventually, you have to "feel" it. You can't think about it... If you can't feel it -- you can't do it.*
>
> **Lee Sedgwick and Sue Taft**
> **Erie, Pennsylvania**

If you want to try flying solo, here are a few things to remember:

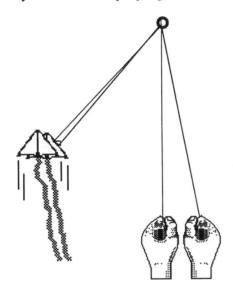

1. Practice by standing out on the edge of the wind. The kite will be moving slower there -- giving you more time to adjust your thinking to this new perspective.

2. Use relatively long lines -- at least 150 feet. When you "bend" your lines through the stake, the distance from the kite to this "pivot" point will only be 75 feet and the kite will move very fast.

3. Forget about thinking "left and right".

Some flyers recommend switching handles so that pulling right will create a right turn. But the experts say that doesn't help. It just makes things <u>more</u> confusing.

4. Stand so that the lines between you and the stake are LONGER than the lines between the stake and the kite. Remember that basic safety rule: don't fly when someone is under your kite or lines -- including yourself!

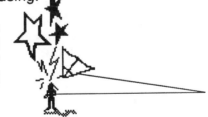

Solo Flying provides some spectacular opportunities for the flyer to interact with their kite. But be warned ... it takes a lot of practice and getting used to.

> *Flylines have a tendency to wear out much more quickly when run around a dog stake. Try treating the line with a Silicone-based spray which is available at many hardware stores. You can also shorten the line occasionally to move the wear point where it rubs against the stake. Finally, choose a stake that is more rounded than angular. Time spent preparing equipment will reduce repairs and replacemnt costs later.*

DUAL FLIGHT

Usually, when we talk about flying multiple kites, we're referring to stacks. Dual Flight is a bit different. Here we're talking about one flyer controlling TWO INDEPENDENT KITES!

But if each kite has two lines and requires two hands to control, how does a flyer maneuver more than one kite??

Dual flyers generally tie two of the four lines to a harness. Some fly one kite with their hips and one with their hands. Others attach the inside line from each kite to their waist and control or maneuver each kite with just one hand. That's the method we'll describe here.

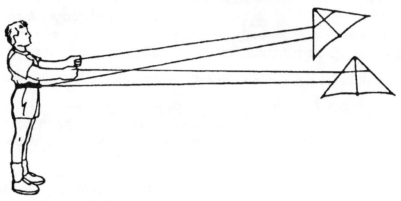

1. Identify one kite as the left kite and one as the right. Then when you set up, tie the two INSIDE lines to your harness. This means that both kites will TURN LEFT when you simultaneously PULL with your LEFT HAND and PUSH with your RIGHT.

2. Make sure the two inside lines are SLIGHTLY LONGER than those on the outside. This allows you some room to push and pull on either side. To fly straight, you cock both arms slightly forward.

3. Tune your kites as you would for a formation or team. This includes adjusting line lengths and moving the clips so both kites fly at the same speed. (See the section on Formation Flying.)

4. Self launches are tough since you have to balance both kites during lift-off. Practice with a helper by launching one kite first, stabilizing, and then launching the second.

5. Since your lines are attached to your waist, you can help your steering by MOVING YOUR HIPS. Try it! Eventually, you may get good enough to fly a third kite on your hips alone.

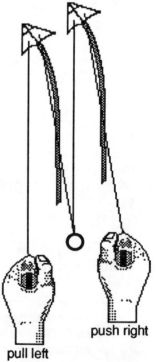

pull left

push right

Dual flying takes a great deal of concentration. It's a lot like rubbing your stomach and patting your head -- each hand needs to be doing something different while you "think about both of them". Like everything else in stunting, improvement takes practice.

"QUAD" FLYING

Most stunt kites operate on two lines which attach to the kite at the bridle clips. By adjusting the position of the clips on the bridle, speed, maneuverability, and responsiveness can be changed. (See the chapter on Tuning.)

The problem, of course, is that once you adjust your clips to one setting, you can't change them until you land the kite again. Imagine what you could do if bridle settings could be changed <u>while the kite is in the air</u>.

"Quad" or four line flying allows you to do just that.

With four lines, you'll find that you can actually stop the kite in the center of the wind, land directly downwind, or even back up. Best of all, you can perform incredibly fast and tight spins. And of course, you can absolutely amaze anyone watching.

DELTA WING QUAD FLYING -- Almost any delta wing stunt kite can be altered for quad line flying. The changes are not permanent and can be made in just a few minutes. All you need are two extra bridle lines and an extra pair of clips.

The length of your new bridle depends on the size of your kite. Experiment! Attach one end at the lower vinyl connector on the leading edge and the other at the base of the Center Strut. All four lines have their own bridle clips and, of course, attach to four separate flylines.

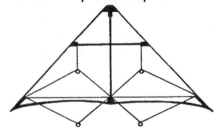

Generally, the kite will handle better if the two upper flylines are slightly longer than the two lower ones. And remember to adjust the original or "old" bridles for a greater angle of attack by moving the clips up.

We learned earlier that small bridle adjustments change the kite's angle of attack -- the angle at which the kite meets the wind.

Now by pulling on the two upper lines, we can make the kite move faster, climb higher and fly farther to the sides of the wind. The upper lines also provide more lift and improve light wind handling. By pulling the lower lines, we can stop, stall, or even move the kite backwards.

top line pulled back

more speed and tighter turns

bottom line pulled back

stall and no lift

Left and right movements or turns are handled just like with a standard bridle. But now you have additional control for speed and sensitivity.

> *Spend some time marking your flylines so you can tell the right from left and the top from the bottom. A little time spent on this can save a whole afternoon of untangling. Also, when you put your lines away, wrap them up in pairs instead of putting all four lines on one holder. Otherwise, you may suffer the curse of a million wraps ... but worse!*
>
> **Lee Sedgwick**
> **Erie, Pennsylvania**

QUAD LINE HANDLES -- At this point, you're probably saying to yourself, "This all sounds like great fun, but what the heck do I do with four flylines?" It's a reasonable question...

to "upper" bridle

For Quad Line flying, you need a special kind of strap or handle that allows you to attach two lines -- one at EACH END.

to "lower" bridle

Remember that to tune a kite, you move the bridle clips only a few inches. Now you can make the same small changes on the upper and lower bridle lines by holding the straps or handles in the palms of your hands and manipulating them by rotating your wrists up and down.

"MADE FOR QUAD LINE" KITES -- Because they were designed primarily for forward flight, most delta style stunt kites are a bit cumbersome when altered for quad flying. They turn faster and change speed easily, but handle backward flight awkwardly. More importantly, most delta wing kites don't have enough sail area to off-set the drag created by four lines.

The new quad liners -- kites specifically designed to utilize four lines -- overcome all of these problems.

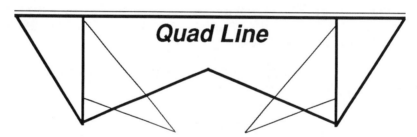

Quad Line

The Made for Quad Line Kites move forward and backward with equal grace. They can hover directly downwind, stop suddenly at any point inside the wind window, and will rotate around their center much like a propeller. But try to fly them like a standard stunter and they will make you crazy.

The key to flying these new kites is to forget almost everything you've learned about "push" and "pull" maneuvering. Try to steer by pulling to the left or right and the air will spill out of the kite and it will flutter to the ground. Instead, you steer the kite by holding your hands together and rotating the handles back and forth with your wrists. Pretend you're wearing handcuffs. Better yet, do wear handcuffs until you get the hang of it. Then you can begin to integrate some very subtle push turns into your performance.

> *Dual and Quad flying both require two sets of line of slightly different lengths. Rather than fill your kite bag with dozens of lines specifically cut and marked for different types of flying, pre-stretch your lines and cut them to identical lengths. Then when you need to adjust for Quad or Dual flying, simply add a short piece of "extender" line to your handles. It's much less confusing and uses a lot less line.*

CHAPTER NINE: CONTEST FLYING

So. You've read the book. You've practiced for hundreds of hours and you know you've got the maneuvers down "pat". In other words, you think you're a pretty "hot" stunt kite pilot.

Ready to find out how you shape up against the competition??

Stunt kite contests are now being held at hundreds of organized events around the country and around the world. Like many sports, competition standards will vary tremendously depending on the scope and seriousness of the event. Some contests are strictly for fun. Some are informal, and some are conducted according to detailed rules and with large money prizes and natitional "titles" at stake. Brace yourself ...

In this chapter, we're going to talk about the contests that are run according to internationally acccepted rules. We'll tell you what specific events are being flown and give you some hints that will add a few points to your score.

If you're ready for events run "by the rules", you'll be ready for anything. Your self-confidence, practice, and ability will prepare you for almost any kind of competition you're likely to encounter.

> *A common rule book for stunt kite competition has now been adopted by the American Kitefliers Association (AKA) for use in the USA, by Stunt Team and Competitive Kiting (STACK) for use in Europe, Australia and New Zealand, and by the All Japan Sport Kite Association (AJSKA) in Japan. Each country hosts a series of events which lead to national titles for individuals and teams. National champions then gather each year for an international competition.*
>
> *For a copy of the AKA/STACK/AJSKA Rule Book, write to the American Kitefliers Association at 1559 Rockville Pike, Rockville Maryland 20852 USA.*

LEVELS OF COMPETITION

The important thing to remember about contests is that, except at the most informal events, contestants are divided into categories based on their experience and ability. You won't have to fly against the "experts" until you've demonstrated that you're ready and able. So relax!

Think of your first competition as an opportunity to learn. Talk to the judges. Ask lots of questions. Find out what you did wrong and also what you did right.

> *Remember, it's your job to know the rules and your job to be in the right place at the right time. Stay informed about what's going on around you. Ask questions if you're unsure. Missing your turn is just like "blowing" a maneuver. You have no one to blame but yourself.*
>
> *Eric Forsberg*
> *Forest Grove, Oregon*

> *"Competitive Fever" -- That's what you get when you first step onto the contest flying field. You can practice for hours and be REALLY good. But step out in front of a crowd and judges, and suddenly you start acting like a rank amateur and do some of the dumbest things!*
>
> *The best way to cure competitive fever is to COMPETE. Some people never get over the stage fright - but the more you compete, the less it bothers you.*
>
> **Al Hargus III**
> **Chicago, Illinois**

Here is a breakdown on the different categories or classes of flyers:

Novice -- A competition beginner who has not won or placed in previous events or does not feel ready to compete in a higher class. Many large scale stunt kite events do not include a Novice competition.

Intermediate -- For flyers who have won or placed in Novice or feel ready to compete at a higher level.

Experienced -- Flyers who have competition experience, good mastery of flying techniques and a higher skill level than the majority of Intermediate flyers.

Masters -- For competitors who have won events in lower classes and feel that they have the necessary skills and experience to compete among the very best.

Open -- Open to all flyers, regardless of the classes that they fly in other events.

Teams -- Teams comprised of flyers with mixed skill levels are ranked by averaging. A three person team with two Experienced and one Masters flyer may fly Experienced Class; a three person team with one Experienced and two Masters flyers must fly Masters Class. If equal numbers of flyers have the same skill level the team competes in the higher class.

Generally speaking, competitors have the option of moving "up" at any time. But once you compete at a higher level, you have to stay there.

Flyers can compete at the same level throughout an entire competition season. But if they place first, second, or third, three or more times in a year, they have to move to the higher classification at the begining of the next season.

> *When gearing up for that big event, work out all the details of your routine, and work on that routine in all wind conditions. Remember, contests aren't always held in perfect wind.*
>
> *Put your ideas on paper, and refer to the diagrams frequently. "Plan your fly, and fly your plan." Rehearse until you know the routine by heart. Rehearse until you impress yourself! But also allow some degree of flexibility for those unfortunate and unforeseen circumstances.*
>
> **Bob Hanson**
> **Sea Bright, New Jersey**

Editor's Note: Special thanks to The "No Secrets" Newsletter by Dragons and Butterfles Productions for tips and hints listed in this Chapter.

HOW A COMPETITION WORKS

Stunt kite competitions are conducted on marked flying fields. Boundaries are outlined to give the competitors plenty of clear and open space to perform and to keep spectators safely outside the flying area. Individuals or teams then come onto the field in a pre-arranged order to perform.

The most efficiently run contests rely on a "Stage-In" Field, a "Competition" Field and a "Stage-Out" Field. Some also provide a practice area.

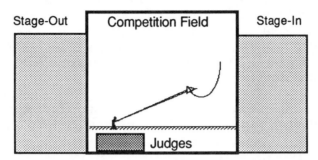

Flyers set-up and launch on the Stage-In field, move to the Competition field when they are called, and then move off to the Stage-Out field and land after their performance. This process reduces the time used for set-up during a contest and keeps things moving along. Competition fields are usually 200-300 feet square.

> *Whatever event you enter, be it Team, Individual Ballet, Precision, or whatever, you HAVE TO do it inside the boundaries of the contest field. The size of the field may vary at different contests, but the rules are -- if you go out of bounds, you get disqualified.*
>
> *It doesn't matter if the winds are light. You aren't allowed to back-up off the field to stay airborne. If the winds are strong and you get pulled out -- too bad... In competition, you have to do it in the flagged-off field. Period.*
>
> **Al Hargus III**
> **Chicago, Illinois**

A number of personnel are needed to keep the contest organized, fair, and safe. Fortunately, you only need to worry about a few of them.

> **Announcer --** Uses the public address system to announce the order or location of events, summon contestants to the Stage-In field, and promote safety. Also announces results and keeps spectators informed.
>
> **Pit Boss --** Controls the Stage-In field. Maintains flight order, tells flyers where to launch and directs them to the Field Director when it is time to compete. <u>Always</u> stay in contact with the Pit Boss so you don't miss your turn.
>
> **Field Director --** Runs the Competition field. Tells judges when contestants are ready for each required maneuver or program. Has diagrams of compulsory figures. Times all events and coordinates field safety. Informs pilot if they have gone over boundaries or run out of time. If you have questions, ask the Field Director.
>
> **Judges --** Rate each flyer's performance. Usually, at least three judges review an event. If more judges are used, high and low scores will be disgarded before averaging.

There are two other things you need to know about formal stunt kite contests.

A **Pilot's Meeting** is generally held before each event. Contestants should attend to find out any last minute changes, how the event will be run, and their flying order. If you miss the Pilot's Meeting, you risk missing important information or changes.

All events operate under a **Wind Rule**. Actually, there are two rules: one for <u>minimum speed</u> and one for <u>maximum speed</u>. If the wind drops below the point where the judges feel flyers can adequately perform (6 m.p.h. for Novice, 5 for Experienced, and 3 m.p.h. for Open Class), a recess, changes in required figures, or other rule changes may be announced. The same goes for high winds (20 m.p.h. for Novice and 30 for Experienced and Open Class).

Of course, at some point, the "show must go on". At that point, minimum and maximum speed go out the door and the only rule remaining is **"fly or die"**. So if you want to win, be ready to perform in any conditions.

TYPES OF EVENTS

Contests currently focus on two basic categories: Precision and Choreography or "Ballet". Either category can be performed by individuals or by teams.

Precision -- Precision competition for individuals and teams is designed to test your <u>technical flying ability</u>. The rule book illustrates a number of precision figures. Event organizers pick between three and five "compulsory maneuvers" from the book and judge you on how well you can do them.

Compulsory figures are designed to test flying skill and precision in execution. Corners should be nintey degrees sharp or circles fully round. Scores will depend on how closely a figure matches the book diagrams - including direction. Speed through each maneuver should also remain constant, so remember what you learned about throttle control.

Usually, the compulsories are announced before the event and you can practice them. Other surprise figures may be announced at the pilot's meeting. Examine all the figures carefully. If you fly something wrong, backwards, start at the wrong place, or leave something out, your score will reflect it.

Precision contests may also provide a two-three minute period for freestyle maneuvers. This is your opportunity to fly any maneuvers you like. Judges will be looking for the <u>variety and difficulty</u> of maneuvers, and the perfection with which you fly them. Showing a greater number of maneuvers, choosing maneuvers that are relatively more difficult, showing excellence in their execution, and planning the routine to "flow" from beginning to end will all contribute to a higher score.

To improve team performance, concentrate on the basics. Get those down first and then work on the freestyle. Be prepared to make a commitment to the team. A time commitment and a commitment to the level of performance that the team wants to acheive. Keep it fun. If it gets too serious, you'll burn out. And finally, ask questions. Don't be afraid to ask the top flyers. They love the sport and want to keep it alive.

If you're looking for a few extra points in Precision, remember these tips:

-- Know the required compulsaries. If you don't understand something,ask the Field Director or at the Pilot's Meeting.
-- Don't begin any maneuver until the Field Director tells you the judges are ready.
-- When the judges are ready, begin your maneuver as soon as possible. Bored judges give low scores.
-- Knowledgeable flyers call "IN" when they begin a maneuver and "OUT" when they finish it. Say it loud enough for the judges to hear.
-- In freestyle, strive to impress the judges with your technical expertise. Try flying the compulsary maneuvers for the next higher class.
-- If you crash before the minimum time limit in freestyle, you must relaunch to get any points. If you see a crash is coming, and you've made it past the minimum time, call "OUT". The judges won't count the crash.
-- If you're having trouble with light or heavy winds, cut your freestyle short. Judges don't deduct points for short routines.
-- If you're going to attempt a risky maneuver, save it for the end.

> *To maximize points in Precision, fly big, fly slow, and make your transitions flow. Also, call "In" and "Out" as though the judges were standing in Northern Quebec.*
>
> *By flying large maneuvers, you give the judges a chance to really see the move you're doing. Too often, pilots zip through a performance, and the judges are left to wonder whether or not the maneuver was done well. Remember, there is no time limit for compulsories!*
>
> *The real key to winning in the freestyle segment of a program is a smooth, flowing transition from one move to another. Almost any pilot can fly the precision moves. Demonstrate a sense of planning and foresight in your routine. I try to enter a new figure in the same area of the sky where the last figure stopped, so that there are no wild or wasted moments setting up one move to another.*
>
> **Bob Hanson**
> **Sea Bright, New Jersey**

Choreography or Ballet -- Ballet competition for both individuals and teams focuses on technical skill and flying artistry. Flyers perform free style flight to the music of their choice. A small part of the score is reserved for music selection. You provide a cassette tape.

Music should be appropriate for kite ballet, having variations in mood and tempo that allows creativity and variety. Maneuvers should be timed and executed to the music. Judges consider the number and quality of maneuvers based on execution, positioning, smoothness, degree of difficulty and the utilization of the "wind window".

Here are your tips for improving ballet performance:

-- Make sure you have handed in your tape and that it is properly cued and marked "This side up".
-- Watch out for songs with very quiet parts. Many P.A. systems won't broadcast it effectively.
-- Bring a back-up tape just in case something goes wrong.
-- If the sound crew does start the tape in the wrong place, ask the Field Director for a new start.
-- You don't need to use the full amount of time. Again, bored judges give low scores.
-- Remember that performances vary with wind conditions. Be flexible enough to alter your plans if the wind won't let you keep up with your music.

> *Entertainment is the primary objective of any ballet performance. The key is to produce an emotional response from the judges and the crowd. Most classical music or movie themes work well because they are designed to evoke emotions.*
>
> *Within any routine, I try to generate anticipation, surprise, and tranquility. Tranquilty comes from experiencing soft flowing music as the kite floats through graceful turns. Anticipation can be achieved by flying the kite on a collision course with the ground or other kites as the music reaches a climax. Surprise is created when the kite does something unexpected - like not crashing.*
>
> *I try to keep routines fairly short and not risk creating another emotion -- boredom.*
>
> **Ron Reich**
> **San Diego, California**

Other Events -- Competitions are expanding to include a number of new or developing categories. Here are a few examples:

Innovative -- In this event you can try almost anything. Music is optional and there is no restriction on kites other than safety. Quad line, dual flying and dog stakes all fit in Innovative. You can even switch kites during your performance.

Train Ballet -- Stacks have their own unique appeal and beauty but often have difficulty completing technical maneuvers. The Train Ballet category allows you to compete against other stacks instead of single kites.

Pairs Competition -- It is difficult for a two-person team to compete against three, four or five flyers. The intricacy of multi-kite maneuvers places a pair at a clear disadvantage. In Pairs Comptition, only two-person teams compete.

General Competition Suggestions -- No matter what category or event you enter, there are basic tips that will help you do better and have more fun:

-- Practice in as many different wind conditions as possible.
-- Check your equipment and tuning before you compete. Don't rely on new or unfamiliar kites and line.
-- Watch the contestants ahead of you to see what the wind is doing.
-- Make sure the Pit Boss knows who you are and where you are.
-- Be ready to go when it's you're turn. Never keep the judges waiting.
-- Recruit a good relaunch crew. No one plans to crash. And remember to brief your crew so they know what you want done.
-- If you do crash, stay calm. If it's a musical event, keep track of the song so you can get back into your routine as soon as you relaunch.
-- Think positive! Don't be nervous. If you say, "I'm gonna crash!" you probably will. Fly to please yourself and you'll always do your best.
-- Accept bad breaks graciously. Be a good sport. Congratulate the people that beat you and always thank the judges and field crew.
-- Learn from everything - good and bad -that happens on the field.
-- Enjoy yourself! Enjoy yourself! Enjoy yourself!

Competitive flying is an excellent way to test your skill and improve your ability. The best advice we can give you is to PRACTICE. Study your maneuvers, know the rules, and watch the other flyers for new ideas. Then PRACTICE MORE.

Like we've been saying all along, <u>finesse, precision, and delicacy of control</u> distinguish an expert stunt kite pilot. Good Luck!

Conclusion

We hope we've been able to communicate our sense of joy and wonder at what stunt kites offer. Sometimes it's hard to explain to people until they see a grown man or woman out there on the flying field with that uniquely silly grin on their face.

If, through our stunt kite manual, you've learned to fly safer, better, or skipped over a few problems that you might have otherwise encountered, than we've accomplished our goal.

All we ask in return is that you pass your experience along to the next new flyer you meet.

The sensation of flying kites is not the only reward that the stunt kite sport has brought to us. We've also been privileged to meet new and warm friends all around the globe.

Occasionally, we are flattered at an event when a winning competetor turns and says, "I learned to fly from your book." Other times, the introduction is a bit more of a reality check -- like when people come up and say, "You must be the Gombergs. We recognized the dog from the cover!"

Either way, please make a point of saying hello if our paths ever cross. Let us know what you thought of our book.

And if someday you win the Grand Nationals or the World Cup, please remember to send us your autograph!

Come fly with us!

Join the worldwide membership of the
AMERICAN KITEFLIERS ASSOCIATION

◆ Bimonthly Newsletter *Kiting* with Kitevents Calendar, Kite Plans, Chapter Activities, Regional Reports and More ◆ 10% Discount from Member Merchants ◆ $100,000 Liability Insurance Any Time You Fly ◆ Membership Directory and Factbook ◆ Manuals and Informational Publications ◆ $1,000,000 Liability Insurance at Sanctioned Events ◆ Local Club Assistance ◆ Annual Convention, Kite Auction, and Grand National Competition ◆

AKA • 1559 Rockville Pike, Rockville, MD 20852-1651 • USA

Fly safely!

- Never fly in wet or stormy weather.
- Never fly near power lines, and do not try to free a kite caught in a power line—call the power company.
- Never use metallic flying line.
- Do not fly near trees, streets, or airports.
- Fly on a field free of potholes & debris.
- Do not allow your kite or line to touch any bystander.
- Wear gloves and use extreme caution with large kites; never leave them unattended.
- Do not fasten yourself to your line unless you have a quick release mechanism.
- Be particularly careful with stunt kites. Make sure your flying area is clear, and never fly over spectators.

MEMBERSHIP APPLICATION

12/91

- ☐ NEW MEMBERSHIP
- ☐ RENEWAL
- ☐ REINSTATEMENT

- ☐ I wish to register as a Member Merchant
- ☐ Do not publish my name in the AKA Directory
- ☐ Do not distribute my name outside AKA

NAME		SPOUSE	
ADDRESS			
CITY		STATE	ZIP
PHONE (H) ( )		PHONE (W) ( )	
NAMES OF OTHER FAMILY MEMBERS			
CHARGE TO MY VISA / MASTER CARD #			EXPIRES
SIGNATURE			

My primary interest is: ☐ Single-Line Kites   ☐ Multi-Line Kites   ☐ All Kinds of Kites

Referred by _____   My local club: _____

Membership Dues	1 YR	2 YR	3 YR	AMOUNT
SPONSOR *KITING via 1st Class Mail* (INCLUDES TAX-DEDUCTIBLE CONTRIBUTION)	100.	200.	300.	_____
INDIVIDUAL *KITING via 3rd Class Mail*	20.	39.	56.	_____
FAMILY ASSOCIATE *per person* (ADDITIONAL FAMILY MEMBERS IN SAME HOUSEHOLD)	4.	8.	12.	_____
US 1st CLASS MAIL *add*	8.	15.	22.	_____

International Members please add postage as follows:

CANADA/MEXICO	8.	15.	22.	_____
OVERSEAS SURFACE MAIL	10.	19.	28.	_____
OVERSEAS AIR MAIL	25.	48.	70.	_____

TOTAL REMITTANCE _____

PLEASE REMIT IN U.S. DOLLARS.
SORRY, WE CANNOT TAKE CANADIAN CHEQUE

Send this form with your payment to
AMERICAN KITEFLIERS ASSOCIATION
1559 Rockville Pike • Rockville, MD 20852-1651 • USA
(800) AKA-2550 • (408) 647-8483